Swimming
the SHANE
GOULD
WAY

Shane, aged 15 years and three weeks, has just broken the 1500-metre world record.

Swimming the
SHANE GOULD WAY

BY SHIRLEY GOULD

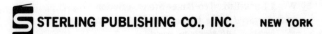

STERLING PUBLISHING CO., INC.   NEW YORK

Oak Tree Press Co., Ltd.
London

DEDICATION

To my four daughters
Lynette, Shane, Debbie and Jenny
and my husband, Ron.

ACKNOWLEDGMENTS

Grateful acknowledgment is made to Forbes Carlile, who took all of the underwater photographs, and to Tom Green for technical comment and encouragement. Thanks are also due to my brother, Barry C. Reid, for permission to use photographs originally intended for Shane to analyze her own stroke technique; and to Tony Duffy of London and the *Sydney Morning Herald* for the use of their photographs. Thanks also to Jas. Clarke & Co. Ltd., for use of the hymn lines from "Just As I Am," by Marianne Farningham.

Copyright © 1972 by Shirley Gould
Published by Sterling Publishing Co., Inc.
419 Park Avenue South, New York, N.Y. 10016
British edition published by Oak Tree Press Co., Ltd., Nassau, Bahamas
Distributed in Australia by Oak Tree Press Co., Ltd.,
P.O. Box 34, Brickfield Hill, Sydney 2000, N.S.W.
Distributed in the United Kingdom and elsewhere in the British Commonwealth
by Ward Lock Ltd., 116 Baker Street, London W 1
Manufactured in the United States of America
All rights reserved
Library of Congress Catalog Card No.: 72-81034
ISBN 0–8069- 4056 –5   UK 7061–2375–1
4057 –3

CONTENTS

Mr. S. B. Grange

Foreword

The greatest swimmer Australia has produced, and indeed the world has seen, is Shane Gould who on the 8th January, 1972, at the age of 15 years swam 100 metres in 58.5 seconds and consolidated her claim to every world's freestyle swimming record for women.

This achievement came after successful tours of England, Europe and the United States as a result of which she has been awarded almost every known sporting trophy, both at home and abroad, which recognizes outstanding athletic achievements.

Despite her fame, Shane is still a modest girl, who has deep affection and respect for her family. It is against this background and with a desire to help other swimmers that her mother decided to write the story of Shane's career.

In preparing swimmers, the modern coach draws upon many sciences—physics, body mechanics, nutrition, psychology and anatomy are some which are continually applied in any programme.

Shirley Gould is not a coach but essentially an intelligent and observant mother who knows instinctively what motivates her daughter's resolute approach to the sport and, as I see it, this is the purpose of the book.

—Syd Grange, O.B.E., M.V.O.,

Bureau Member,

Federation Internationale de Natation Amateur

Celebrities from all over the world have been thrilled by Shane Gould's spectacular breaking of all five world records for women. Here Bing Crosby congratulates Shane.

1. "A Love Affair with the Water"

Shane's love affair with the water began before she could walk. As a baby she cried when bath-time ended; she crawled down the beach straight into the waves of Sydney Harbour; she bobbed about in a rubber tyre smiling with satisfaction before she was a year old. She always had complete confidence when in the water and was probably retarded in learning to swim by her parents' being anxious about her taking risks in the water.

Before she was 3 she could swim under-water with eyes open, and soon after she turned 3 she was managing a respectable dog paddle. At 5 she was a small expert at snorkel and mask around the reefs of Fiji, where we had moved, and at 6 she had her first lessons from a professional swimming coach, New Zealander, Paul Krause. By 8 she was reasonably proficient in all swimming strokes except the butterfly, which she had heard about but had never seen. At 9 we moved back to Sydney and she joined a squad being coached by Ken Wiles of Sans Souci. A month later (January, 1966) she was in her first competition, and won a silver medal for second place in the under-10 division of breaststroke in the New South Wales Swimming Championships.

Shane, 15 years old as this is being written, has been called the greatest woman swimmer in the world today. What makes her swim? How does she do it? What meaning does it have for her? These are some of the questions I have tried to answer—through my observations and relationship with my daughter Shane.

Shane, three years old wearing a mask and inflatable ring, lines up with her older sister, Lynette, and her father for an "underwater adventure" on a small island off Fiji.

WHAT SWIMMING MEANS TO SHANE

Shane has a very special sense of joy when in the water—a sensuous delight in the buoyancy and semi-weightlessness provided by the water, and a fulfilled delight in feeling that she has mastery over it.

A swimming pool provides a world of challenge and demands an individual response from her. Each pool has a "character" of its own: variation in temperature, depth, concentration of chlorine or salt, painted markings on the bottom of the pool, height of the wall, the amount of wind, sun glare or dazzle of lights. All have significance for her, and all in some way evoke a special response from her—a subsequent bid to become mistress over these particular challenges.

Some swimmers are said to "fight the water." But Shane moves through it as if the water itself is propelling her. "I felt right in the water today" she comments simply. "Right" means that she felt at one with the water; it was a friend to be worked with co-operatively.

The Ryde swimming pool in Sydney on a cold morning (water 65° F).
Shane is on the far left.

Her technique makes use of the water and she swims with a flowing, lyrical movement and consummate ease.

Swimming to Shane is a beautifully satisfying sensation. While she doesn't fight the water it does tend to control her movements, yet she also controls the water, which after all is not a human's natural element. Shane has made it hers.

2. Physiology and Personality

Shane's body shape seems almost designed for slipping through the water in the smoothest possible way. She is "streamlined"—tall, slim, strong at the shoulders, tapered at the hips and legs, without much fat, and of course her muscle-to-weight ratio has been developed by training.

In addition to having the "right" shape, she has an extraordinary degree of physical co-ordination. She is an expert ball handler, and learns skills based on hand-eye co-ordination very rapidly. In swimming, this means that arms, legs, breathing, position of body and so on all combine into a graceful and powerful symphony of movement. She is very healthy and very fit. For example, her originally low heart-rate of 60 beats has been lowered to 40—and sometimes still lower—by her having gone through intensive training, causing less strain on her heart during a race.

Coaches have all commented on how easy she is to teach. She manages to grasp quickly what is suggested for improvement. She has learnt and incorporated into her swimming something from each of the seven coaches who have taught her. Coming "late" (at 13 years) to coach Forbes Carlile she was fascinated by his scientist's approach to swimming, and by then she was ready herself to make swimming a serious matter. Earlier, swimming had been a fairly light-hearted affair, sandwiched in amongst other sporting activities. At 13 she knew what her talent was and was quite prepared to leave other interests behind in order to see how far she could get in the swimming world. Keeping a log book (see Chapter 7), setting her own alarm for early morning training, watching her diet—all these were

Lynette (9), Shane (7) at Collaroy, one of Sydney's Northern beaches. Even at this age Shane had the wide shoulders and slim physique essential for a potential champion swimmer.

new and exciting experiences for her, and she tackled them with determination and enthusiasm.

"Shane seems to have the right temperament for competitive swimming," is a comment I have heard more times than I could count. I believe that excellence in any field is achieved by working at it consistently and hard—and for Shane it's in swimming. A "doer" rather than a "talker," she has a real ability for getting on with any job and completing it. Her perseverance seems at times to reach the point of perseveration or continuous repetition in her desire to master a new physical skill. Tree climbing, high jumping, horse riding, basketball, skimboard and surfboard riding—all have been tried by Shane with grit and determination. Each new challenge demands a different set of muscles. The sustained effort needed for perfection has left her sore and complaining for days afterwards. The result has been that she then needs massage, ray lamp, and sympathy. But the shining eyes of "I did it, Mum" more than compensate for her discomfort and the need for parental ministrations!

As for competition, Shane regards it purely as a challenge to herself. When she was about 10, she saw racing as measuring herself against someone else's ability, but by 13 she saw it as a chance to improve herself. Race times then only became important to her if she was out to break her own, personal records.

EXCITEMENT vs. NERVOUSNESS

Prior to races, she gets excited but not nervous. Excitement is a positive emotion—it stimulates adrenalin and brings out the best effort. Excessive nervousness is destructive and it's saddening to see a competitor so weak from this crippling feeling that she is unable to do her best.

Shane is actually exhilarated by racing. The lesson learnt in swimming—that those who have trained well will probably race well—has carried over into other departments of life, notably schoolwork. She tries hard to keep up with school requirements and she almost enjoys the prospect of an examination if she feels sure she has done enough work beforehand. Confidence in her own ability to perform well under pressure has been a real gain to her personality development.

Through swimming, Shane has reached the position of success where she could call herself a citizen of the world. She is accepted immediately into any of the countries where swimming is a national sport. At home she is happiest amongst her "peer" group, which is the cream of Australia's swimmers. Since she entered the National Championship class she has made warm friends amongst swimmers, officials and fans in every state in Australia, and in Europe and California also.

Family? Oh yes, we have encouraged her, happy to

Talking to the coach right after the race is a good idea, because valuable thoughts may later be forgotten. Coach Forbes Carlile was obviously pleased with Shane's performance in this race (the record 100 metres in 58.5 sec).

see her "doing her thing" until she has become the best in the world at it. But also, alongside the encouragement has been this directive: we want her to give it up as soon as the sport of swimming ceases to be fun to her.

SHANE'S SWIMMING-TRAINING

In July, 1970, when, for reasons of her father's employment, our family moved from Brisbane to Sydney, Shane was tearfully heartbroken about leaving the Fortitude Swimming Club, and her training squad under the coaching guidance of Gordon Petersen. She had made friends with the boys and girls of the squad, she loved the warm climate of Brisbane, and she was beginning to earn recognition as a swimmer of promise. In planning the move to Sydney, she bargained strongly with us. First, she wanted to join coach Forbes Carlile's squad; second, she hoped we could find a place to live somewhere between the 25m-pool at Pymble and the

50m-pool at Ryde—7 miles away; third, she assured us that she would make getting up early in the morning for swimming-training her responsibility, not ours. She won us over on the three counts!

At that time, the Carlile squad had provided no less than seven swimmers for the Australian team for the Commonwealth Games in Edinburgh. Karen Moras (the 800m world-record holder), Diana Rickard (medley and backstroke), Gail Neall (medley), Jane Comerford (butterfly), Buddy Portier (medley and breaststroke), Paul Jarvie (breaststroke) and Nigel Cluer, who was actually representing New Guinea, but had trained with Carlile. All were swimmers who earned Shane's respect for their performances—all were either Australian title-holders or record-holders.

Shane commenced training while the others were away at the Commonwealth Games, and she put everything she had into the effort to make herself as competent and as fit as they were. She was content with her tiredness, satisfied with sore muscles, and thoroughly confident about having chosen the right squad to join. She kept to her bargain of getting herself up in the morning, and defended the coach's instructions when we queried them.

Her attitude was whole-heartedly positive. She wanted to train hard, and was prepared to accept the readjustment to very early nights and very early mornings. It was to be expected that her enthusiasm would occasionally wane or waver. At these times we suggested that she might like to give it up, but the power of this negative suggestion seemed to re-fire her keenness. For nearly two years now Shane's aims for herself in swimming have been totally hers, within her own psyche. The decision and the commitment have been hers alone.

3. The Freestyle

(Photos FS 1-40 show how this stroke is performed.)

It is extremely hard for a swimmer to describe how he or she swims, as training makes the movements automatic. So the following descriptions are accounts of the four swimming strokes starting with freestyle, as I see Shane swimming them. Her methods may not be best for another person of differing body shape or co-ordination, but they are her own style, as it evolved and was refined by expert coaching. Any good swimmer wishing to become a racer can probably learn from these descriptions of strokes, but probably needs coaching as well.

Freestyle (or the crawl, as it used to be called) is Shane's favourite stroke, and the one at which she has had most success. Seeing her swimming alone, one gets the impression of apparent nonchalance, while noting the smooth arm strokes, a minimal amount of splashing and legs that seem to trail. Shane seems to have elim-inated all wasteful movement and overcome the water's resistance by her powerful, smooth, precise, rhythmic technique which results in great speed.

POSITION IN THE WATER

Shane likes to have the sensation of swimming over the top of the water, and feeling the surge of water rushing past underneath her. She knows she is swimming well if she has this feeling of being light, and not dragged down. The unpleasant sensation of feeling flat or heavy in the water comes when she is tired, has had too heavy a meal, or her stroke is incorrect.

After watching moving pictures of herself swimming, she admits that she doesn't really "hydroplane" over the water, but she goes through it very close to the surface, with shoulders and back (almost to the waist) above the water. The sensation of feeling that she is skimming the surface of the water is a guide to her personally as to how well she is swimming.

Her legs are a little below water—she holds them in a fairly straight position, but they are never really tense. Her heels break the surface of the water when she kicks, her toes always submerged. She turns her head to the side in a very economical movement and breathes in the hollow of the "bow" wave which she sends out in front of her.

ARM ACTION

Entry . . . Her hand goes into the water at about a 30° angle, and is directly in front of its own shoulder. It hits the water on the tips of the fingers, and glides in a little way without tensing or pulling. At this point she begins to kick with the opposite leg.

Pull . . . When her hand has glided in, it starts to pull. Her elbow is up, higher than her hand. She can feel the whole of her arm being used against the resistance of the water. Her pull is conducted in a horizontal fashion, not downwards. It follows the course of a narrow, wavy "S" across the pulling arm's half of the body. Her hand doesn't turn across the centre line of her body, as this would lower her elbow and weaken the pull.

Push . . . When her hand reaches her hip, the wavy pull is completed, and she gives a hard, short, flat-handed push before lifting her arm above the water.

Recovery . . . Her elbow is up, higher than her hand. If it is too high, she feels a strain on her shoulder and she has a tendency to roll over, off balance. She knows herself if her elbow is too high or too low, but if it is just a little wrong in either direction, she needs her coach to judge it and correct it for her. Her hand is

Shane demonstrates the freestyle stroke for her sisters. The photos show more how Shane thinks she swims in the water than what actually occurs.

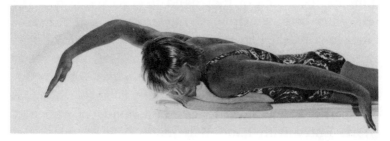

FS 1. Shane's hand goes into the water at an angle of about 30°, directly in front of her shoulder.

FS 2. As soon as her hand has glided in, it starts to pull.

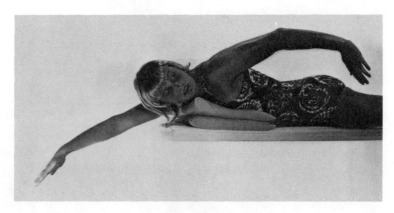

FS 3. Her pull is horizontal.

relaxed but alert and ready for action as it enters into the water. If her hand is too tense, she finds she is thinking too much of that hand to the exclusion of the rest of her body which is, of course, working at the same time. Ideally, she likes her whole body to feel the same— alert for action, nothing tense—each part of her body waiting to pull and push against the water when resistance is offered. Her hand is especially relaxed when it is out of the water, and this allows a saving of muscular effort. Entry with hand B is made before arm A has completed its stroke.

FINGERS

Her fingers are a little bit spaced apart during the pulling. She doesn't use a tightly-held hand like a "scoop"—she prefers to let some water through her fingers. The only time her fingers are closed together is at the point when she gives the flat-handed hard push at the hip. Even then, her thumb is not pressed hard against the other fingers.

FS 4. Shane keeps her fingers loosely apart, not in a tight scoop.

FS 5. Her right arm has almost finished its pull and the left elbow has started up.

FS 6. Her left hand gets ready for entry.

FS 7. As her left hand enters, her right hand is ready to push.

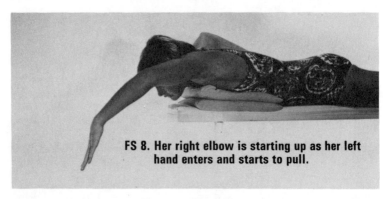

FS 8. Her right elbow is starting up as her left hand enters and starts to pull.

FS 9. Left arm in middle of the pull. Actually, Shane's hand never goes so deep and her elbow never comes up so high.

BREATHING

This part of swimming has to become so automatic for a good swimmer that one is well advised to learn the basics of breathing even before perfecting arm and leg actions. Briefly, breathing-out is done under the water, and breathing-in when the head is turned above the water. The inhaling is rapid and through the mouth, and the exhaling is slow and gradual during the relatively longer time that the face is below water. Shane breathes so that her head moves only to the side. Lifting the head has a slowing effect by creating more water resistance.

In her squad—and this is fairly general in all good Australian swimming squads—the coach insists that all swimmers practise bilateral breathing. This is taking a breath on every third arm stroke so that they breathe on alternate sides. The advantages are considerable. This type of breathing is used as a means of stroke correction to even up each arm stroke; it also causes less slowing down from the breathing action. In a race, there is another advantage—the swimmer never has a "blind" side—he or she can see exactly how the "field" is on either side. The economy of it is seen when you consider that Shane, doing approximately 54 arm strokes in a 50-metre pool would breathe 27 times using unilateral breathing, but only 18 times using the bilateral method.

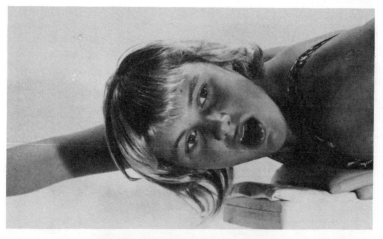

FS 10. Breathing every third arm stroke allows you to take breath on alternate sides, to left, then right. It causes less slowing down and prevents having a "blind" side.

FS 11. Shane imagines she is swimming over the top of the water. This makes her feel light and not dragged down.

FS 12. Breathing to her right side this time, Shane lifts her elbow a little higher than her hand.

THE KICK

Her coach, Forbes Carlile, and other experts describe her kick as a pure "two-beat". This means she gives one kick for each arm stroke with no cross-over action, and it occurs when she is doing her "wavery S" pull. Her kick is, of course, with the opposite leg to the pulling arm, and takes its cue from what the arms are doing, not the other way round. The two-beat kick has been used by a good many swimmers in long-distance races. Shane uses it in sprints too—the first one to do this, I believe.

Some people have commented that she has a "lazy" kick and that her legs simply trail or act as balancing devices. It may seem this way, but Shane is certain that her legs work very hard, as at the end of a race her legs, rather than her arms, feel sore and strained! All the groups of muscles in her ankle, calf and thigh work together in her kicking action. She bends her legs at the knees very slightly, and throughout her swimming carries her legs at the same level below the water.

FS 13. Shane's legs are only a little below the water, and fairly straight but not tense.

FS 14. At entry, her face submerges, and her elbow is kept high.

FS 15. Entry with her right hand is made at the 30° angle.

FS 16. Her legs seem to trail but they are performing a two-beat.

FS 17. When Shane is swimming fast she stirs up very little splash.

FS 18. She glides through the water with all wasteful movement eliminated.

FS 19. Motion picture film shows the details of Shane's freestyle stroke. The series begins during the right arm's pull. She has just taken a breath on the right side.

FS 20. The leg kick is the two-beat. Shane uses it for long-distance racing and—more important—for sprints.

FS 21. Her legs are controlled and strong, but not overly tense.

FS 22. The left arm enters the water just as the right arm begins its recovery.

FS 23. Her right leg is now at the lowest point of the kick. Her left arm has simultaneously begun its pull, and her right hand is pushing.

FS 24. The pull is a "wavery S" as can be seen in this whole series when studied frame by frame.

FS 25. Her left arm comes down under her body about this far only. As these pictures were taken during a training swim, Shane is lower in the water than she would be during a fast race.

TURNING

After a turn at the end of the pool (invariably by the tumble method) she glides out on the strength of the push-off, and when the momentum starts to slow down she gives about ten rapid and vigorous kicks to get up speed until her regular arm and leg strokes can take over. The kick direction is up as well as downwards, and her ankles are always flexible.

FS 26. Shane has just come out of a tumble turn in this series of head-on views. She is still in her glide here.

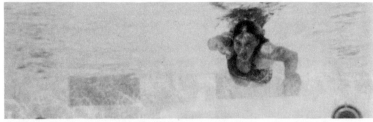

FS 27. As her glide ends, Shane starts her stroke with her right arm.

FS 28. For the pull, she keeps her elbow higher than her hand.

FS 29. Here is the best view of how the recovering arm pulls across half her body.

FS 30. Notice how her position in the water remains steady—no roll from side to side.

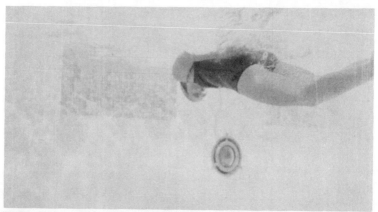

FS 31. The tumble turn is essential for a racing swimmer. Coming in to the wall, Shane's arms are beside her body. She sees the target on the wall through the water.

FS 32. Still a few feet from the wall, she begins her somersault.

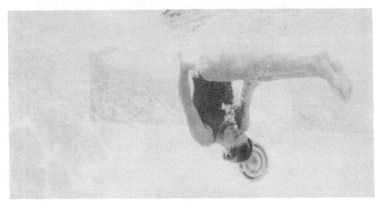

FS 33. Head down, legs parallel to the water line.

FS 34. Her feet will do the touching.

FS 35. Over she goes, feet up now.

FS 36. Her feet near the wall.

FS 37. Now they touch.

FS 38. With a kick, Shane pushes off the wall, throws her arms straight out over her head, and starts her glide. Next position is shown in FS 26.

THE START

When the starter says "take your mark" Shane moves forward and grips the front edge of the block by curling her toes over it. Shane gets ready to start her race by bending forward, arms hanging loosely in front of her legs, feet apart by about 8", and looking ahead, not down.

When "go" is given, her body tenses, arms swing in an upward, outward and finally in a backward direction. Then she brings them rapidly forward, begins to inhale, and pushes off the blocks very strongly. Streamlining her body, she flies straight as an arrow over the water, and enters it at about a 30° angle with fingertips first and the top of her head hitting the surface. Her body continues to glide along under the water on the strength of the dive's propulsion. When this slows to swimming speed, she begins her arm and leg stroke just before her head breaks the surface.

Sometimes Shane's dive does not look like good "text-book" technique. She dives higher than other swimmers who enter the water before she does. Because of this height, she has a more forceful entry into the water and comes up ahead of the other swimmers at the first stroke.

It could be argued that Shane's dive needs to be altered and made lower. On the other hand her unorthodox dive gives her a most effective start, and it may well be the best one for her!

FS 39. Shane starts differently from most racers. She dives higher as can be seen here, but she also comes out farther than the others.

FS 40. Shane enters the water at an angle of only about 10°, but this is ample to prevent a flat start. More on racing starts in the racing section.

WHAT TO AVOID

Shane tries to keep her freestyle as smooth and as even as possible. This means constantly trying to avoid the faults which spoil the smoothness and rhythm. Some of these faults are:

1. Head too high, legs too low—a horizontal position is best.

2. Having the hand enter the water too far away from the body, or coming in across the body. In either of these positions the pull is weakened.

3. Breathing too late so that the arm is held too long in the air on the breathing side. This causes rolling of the body, as one arm will pull longer and stronger than the other.

4. Pulling only with the forearm is wrong. The shoulder muscles and upper arm muscles should be doing their share too.

5. The worst fault is letting the elbow drop so that the entry is first at the elbow and not at the fingers. Coach Forbes Carlile reiterates that the high elbow throughout the pull is of paramount importance. It is interesting to note that all top Australian swimmers feature this characteristic in their style.

4. The Breaststroke

(Photos BR 1-29 show how this stroke is performed.)

Shane has a great fondness for this stroke. It was the first stroke at which she had success in competitive swimming, and she swam it as a "natural" without much instruction. Her stroke was then slow, with very wide arm pull and plenty of glide, but good coaching has altered this so that her stroke now corresponds with the description given here.

As she has worked more on her freestyle, her breaststroke has been set aside to some extent, but it is still a very important stroke for medley swimming. Her best breaststroke time for 100m is 1 min 20 sec and for 200m 2 min 52 sec—both in 50-metre pools.

POSITION IN THE WATER

Fairly horizontal. It is hard for beginners to keep their legs high enough at first. The head at all times (apart from breathing) should be almost completely submerged, with only a "skull cap" of head showing above the water.

BR 1. Shane begins with a glide, her arms outstretched in the water.

ARM ACTION

The stretch. Beginning with a glide, the arms are outstretched in front of the body and about 8″ beneath the surface of the water. The arms are straight and the hands are almost touching. (At this point the legs are also extended.)

The pull. With palms turned outward from the body, the pull is begun, first in a horizontal fashion. The arms then bend at the elbow, while the upper arms remain level with the shoulders, and the pull continues in a downward direction. As with the other strokes, keeping the elbows high gives a better strength of pull.

The recovery. The hands move in towards the chest and then prepare to thrust forward to commence the gliding "stretch." The elbows should not come in and touch the ribs.

BR 2. The pull begins first in a horizontal fashion. Her head begins to lift.

BR 3. Her arms bend at the elbow and the pull continues in a downward direction.

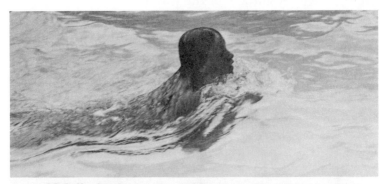

BR 4. Her hands move toward her chest. She takes a breath.

BR 5. Her arms begin the gliding stretch. Her legs prepare to whip together.

THE KICK

Completely different from any of the other strokes, the leg action looks slightly like a frog's kick. Not sharing the frog's leg shape nor his webbed feet, good breaststrokers mostly use the current "whip" kick method.

This kick begins with legs together horizontally, outstretched, and toes pointed. Then the knees bend, bringing the feet back until the heels almost touch the buttocks. The toes then turn outwards, and the soles of the feet face the surface of the water.

Next the feet move outwards, and knees spread apart a little. The legs thrust backwards with a movement that gets faster as the legs are brought together and the legs straighten. This creates the Whip action.

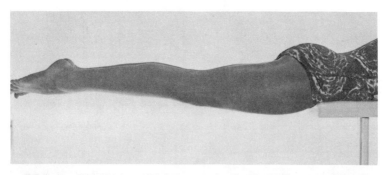

BR 6. Her kick begins with legs together horizontally, toes pointed.

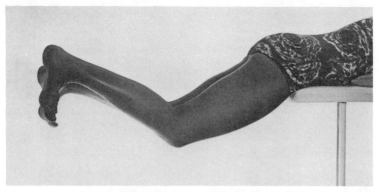

BR 7. How her knees bend.

BR 8. Her heels almost touch her buttocks. Her toes turn outwards, and the soles of her feet face the surface of the water.

BR 9. Her legs are beginning to thrust back now to end completely stretched out as in photo BR 6 on the opposite page.

SYNCHRONIZING ARM AND LEG ACTION

The legs are horizontal for the glide and the strongest part of the pull. The knees start to bend when breathing-in commences, and the "whip" part of the stroke happens when the arms are fully extended. There is a moment of glide when the kick has finished and the arms are stretched out, the body is horizontal and only the top of the crown is above the water.

BR 10. How Shane glides with arms extended past head.

BR 11. Underwater view of Shane gliding.

BR 12. Arms spreading and pulling.

BR 13. Elbows up, whole arm pulling.

BR 14. Arms coming under the body. Shane breathing.

BR 15. Legs beginning to bend at knees, arms bent and in front of chest.

BR 16. Legs bent still more.

BR 17. Legs most bent, arms straightening.

BR 18. Kick starts, feet begin to whip out.

BR 19. Feet whipping out.

BR 20. Legs almost together, arms in glide.

BREATHING

Breathing takes its cue from the arm action. The head begins to lift shortly after the pull begins. Breath is taken as the pull ends and the arms prepare to shoot forward. The head does not lift high—just enough to inhale strongly through the mouth. Pulling the shoulders right out of the water should be avoided as it causes water resistance.

The breath is held from the time the hands are at chest level, during the recovery, until the pull commences. Breathing out under the water is slow, and occurs during the major part of the pulling action.

BR 21. Front view of Shane gliding.

BR 22. Arms spreading.

BR 23. Elbows up. Exhaling.

BR 24. Hands coming up under body. Head above water.

BR 25. Hands up to chest. Breathing through mouth.

BR 26. Arms preparing to shoot forward.

BR 27. Arms going into glide position, legs starting to whip.

BR 28. Legs making whip action.

BR 29. Legs finishing whip, arms almost in glide position.

START AND TURN

The breaststroke dive is a little deeper than in freestyle or in the butterfly, as the swimmer likes to take advantage of the underwater glide and the allowable one arm pull and one leg kick before his head surfaces.

When he turns, he must touch the wall with both hands simultaneously and on the same level, almost exactly as in the butterfly. Pivoting around rapidly to change direction, he pushes off hard and aims to get his glide about 2″ below the water's surface. He glides with arms extended past his head, body streamlined and horizontal. When he feels the strength of the glide lessening, he takes his one arm stroke and his one leg kick before surfacing.

Disqualification occurs more often in breaststroke than in any other stroke. Both sides of the body must function simultaneously and in complete symmetry during the whole swim. If one shoulder drops lower than the other, or one leg kicks lower than the other, or the hands do not touch the wall together at the same level, the swimmer is disqualified—the most disappointing and most frustrating experience a competitive swimmer could ever have.

5. The Butterfly

(Photos BF 1-27 show how this stroke is performed.)

This stroke may be regarded as a double-actioned freestyle. Instead of arms and legs working individually, they function paired and simultaneously. If you think of a horse's gait, then freestyle could be compared with trotting, and butterfly with cantering!

Butterfly is usually the last stroke for a learner to accomplish, because of the muscular strength and co-ordination required. It is particularly hard on the muscles of the shoulders, especially behind the neck, on the upper arms, on the diaphragm and abdomen, and it causes aches in the upper legs. It requires great concentration to keep legs and arms moving in symmetry. While the arms are describing a rough vertical rotation the legs are kicking twice, horizontally.

BREATHING

Some coaches encourage breathing on every stroke. Kevin Berry, previous world-record holder, did this, and some currently outstanding butterfliers still do. Shane usually breathes every second stroke for most of her first lap, and then breathes on every one or two strokes thereafter, depending on how much air she needs. For her last two or three strokes she tries to swim with head down.

The head comes out of the water when the hands are about at the end of the pull and are beginning the push to follow through on the stroke. The feet are just starting to go on the downward part of the kick. As the arms are

BF 1. Breathing-in starts, as Shane's arms begin to come out of the water.

BF 2. Her arms are lifting out in the relaxed recovery position, as breathing-in continues.

BF 3. Breathing-in stops as her head starts to lower, and her arms come rapidly forward.

starting the recovery the breathing is completed, and the feet are at the lowest point of the downward kick. Shoulders should remain low during breathing and the chest should not come out of the water.

Breathing out is done under the water very gradually at the end of the first kick and the beginning of the second, just before raising the head to inhale.

POSITION IN THE WATER

Ideally horizontal, but each section of the body takes its turn at being higher or lower in the water as the arm and leg action causes the characteristic undulating movement. Lacking a strong kick, a swimmer has to use his arms to work harder to compensate for his trunk sinking lower in the water and causing more drag. "Bottoms up," say the beginner's coaches in one squad. "Keep your hips high," say another.

ARM ACTION

The arms come over, out of the water in a relaxed fashion, a little bent at the elbows, and the elbows higher than the wrist. Entry is usually fingertips first, although many good 'fliers enter thumb down. This latter method is generally easier for younger swimmers. The fingers enter approximately at the same angle and position as in freestyle, and the pull travels the similar

BF 4. Her face sinks into the water.

but mirror-imaged wavy-S path under the body, ending the pull with a push.

Learners practising the arm stroke find great benefit in grasping a kick-board between the thighs, as this gives buoyancy to the hips and legs and allows the swimmer to concentrate on getting the arm action right.

BF 5. Her arms begin entry, fingertips first.

BF 6. Her arms begin the pull, which is similar to freestyle.

BF 7. With her arms under water, pulling, Shane gets maximum momentum. The pull ends with a push.

BF 8. Head-on view of the same position as BF 4.

BF 9. Side view of the same position as the hands begin to enter the water.

BF 10. Shane breathes in as her head is entirely out of the water.

BF 11. She has to finish her breathing before her head goes down.

THE KICK

In contrast with freestyle where the legs follow the arms, this stroke depends on the strength of the leg action. Shane, with other Australian butterfly swimmers, uses the double dolphin kick—legs close but not tensely pressed together, with the kick no more than a flexible flick which imitates the dolphin's tail movement.

This is not an easily-grasped action; it needs a lot of perseverance and practice before the muscles are strong enough to do it well. Telling younger children to "wriggle" often gets the message across! Also, learners find that holding a kicking-board out in front of them gives good support to the upper part of the body while the legs are training. (Advanced swimmers also use this for practice.)

The first kick begins when the head is down, the face under the surface of the water, hands entering and arms beginning their pull.

The second kick is stronger: the legs give a forceful slow-motion whip movement downwards, then upwards. The arms come out of the water while the legs are coming up on the kick. The hands enter at the

BF 12. Stroke begins after breath has been inhaled, as hands enter the water.

BF 13. Pull begins at once, legs flicking down.

point of the kick when the feet are breaking the surface of the water, and the knees are bent.

BUTTERFLY DIVE

This is no different from the starting dive for freestyle, but the swimmer begins action with a good strong dolphin kick before he surfaces and starts to do his arm stroke.

BUTTERFLY TURN AND FINISH

To avoid disqualification, it is important to have both hands on the same level of the wall when they

BF 14. Pull continues, legs now down in dolphin style.

BF 15. No question why this is called the butterfly stroke.

BF 16. Here you can see the power of the pull with both arms working simultaneously.

touch for the turn and the finish. After touching, the swimmer bends his legs up under his body, swivels around rapidly, pushes off hard with his feet, glides a little with arms outstretched and body streamlined, gives a dolphin kick, then surfaces and starts his arm pull.

Shane's butterfly is a slow stroke with a powerful pull, and would appear to be most suitable for a good 200m swim. This could be a challenge for her in the future. She herself comments that she lifts out of the water too high for breathing, but she plans to work on eliminating this fault.

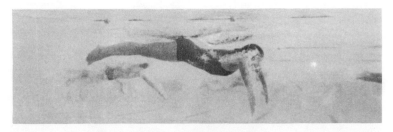

BF 17. Arms go straight down now.

BF 18. Arms give push at end of stroke, as legs start to rise and knees bend.

BF 19. Arms start up again as push is finished.

BF 20. Front view shows head going down and arms about to enter water.

BF 21. Fingertips lead the way into the stroke.

BF 22. Note that the hands move apart as the pull extends outward.

BF 23. Arms are fully apart now and exhaling starts.

BF 24. Arms and hands are pulling strongly now as exhaling continues.

BF 25. Breath is forcefully expelled as elbows now bend on the pull.

BF 26. Stroke is ending, breath is almost all expelled.

BF 27. Shane surfaces for air as her hands push backwards.

6. The Backstroke

(Photos BK 1-30 show how this stroke is performed.)

Shane's backstroke used to be the least efficient stroke in her swimming repertoire: poor shoulder flexibility was possibly the cause of her being somewhat unresponsive to the efforts of her coaches. But improvement is coming, and having a fondness for medley swimming, she is hopeful of better backstroke performance in the future. Her best time for 50m is 34 sec and her best 100m time (in a 25m pool) is 1 min 11.0 sec.

The description which follows is more an account of how Shane would like to swim backstroke than an exact description of her swimming.

ARM ACTION

Recovery . . . The arm, lying along the side of the body, hand near the hip, starts to come up out of the water. The arm is straight but relaxed; the hand, palm down is in line with the arm. The arm lifts high and describes a 180° arc above the water. The whole arm, during the process, gradually rotates so that the palm

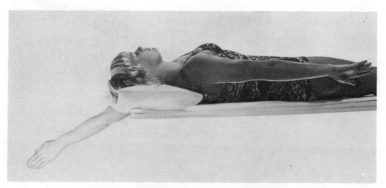

BK 1. Left arm begins pull. Right arm begins recovery.

turns outward, away from the body, and the hand gets ready for the entry. The arm is quite straight during this part of the stroke.

Entry . . . With the palm outwards, the hand can enter, little finger first, in a line directly behind the shoulder belonging to the entering arm. The "karate" edge of the palm slices down into the water for about 10 inches. Fingers are close together but are not stiff. As in freestyle, the pull is weakened if the elbow enters first.

Pull . . . Beginning with a wrist bend, the pull becomes stronger and the elbow bends until the arm is at right angles to the shoulder. As with freestyle, the pull is not a smooth circle, but a wavy movement, shaped like an "S" lying on its side.

Push . . . When the hand finishes the pull at the hips, it changes to a downward pushing movement until the arm is straight again, the hand below the line of the hip. Then the recovery begins again.

The backstroke is an aesthetically pleasing stroke to watch—especially when done by an expert—as the arms move alternately with beautiful symmetry and a constant rhythm. Good backstrokers' arms are always equally distant ("completely opposed") from each other like the blades of a propeller.

BK 2. Right arm rotates so that palm is turning outward.

BK 3. Left arm bends at elbow for pull. Right arm is raised straight up 90°.

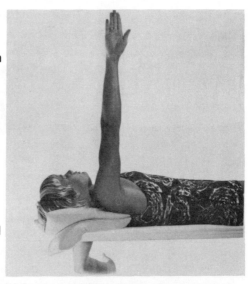

BK 4. Left hand ends pull with push. Right arm reaches out above head, completing 180° arc.

BK 5. Right arm pulls as left arm comes up in relaxed recovery position.

BK 6. Right arm pushes water. Left arm is ready to enter water.

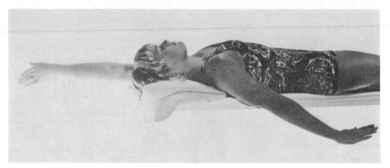

BK 7. Left hand enters water in straight-out position.

POSITION IN THE WATER

The body lies immediately below the surface of the water, the feet lower than the trunk. The face is above water, but the head, including the ears is submerged.

BODY ROLL

In the backstroke, this is a "good thing" in moderation, and the rolling movement should be rhythmically related to the pulling. At the same time, it is important to keep the head steady.

BK 8. Body rides high in the water as right arm starts to come up out of the water.

BK 9. Right arm is relaxed but straight.

BK 10. Palm starts to turn outward as arm raises up 90°.

BK 11. Shane keeps her head steady.

BK 12. Her right hand is getting ready to enter the water, little finger first, palm out.

BK 13. Pulling under water begins with her right arm.

BK 14. Left arm commences recovery.

BK 15. Sequence is repeated with left arm, as right arm pulls under water.

BK 16. Underwater view shows that right hand has entered the water, little finger first. Left hand is below hip.

THE KICK

This is frankly an upside-down version of the freestyle kick. Good backstrokers use a broken tempo, 4-beat or 6-beat flutter kick and, of course, opposite leg and arm work together. There is more bending of the knees than in freestyle, but it is desirable to keep them below the surface of the water. The toes just break the surface of the water.

BK 17. Right hand pulls horizontally as flutter kick begins.

BK 18. Right hand continues to do the work. Knee bends more than in freestyle kick.

BK 19. Now elbow bends sharply. Note position of legs.

Kicking practice is performed with arms extended over the head, thumbs locked together and hips held high in the water.

BK 20. Hard push downwards ends right hand stroke.

BK 21. Left hand enters water as right hand finishes push.

BK 22. Right hand starts recovery. Legs continue flutter kick.

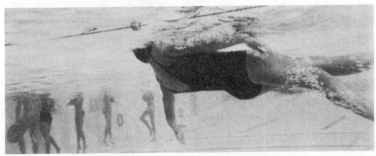

BK 23. Right hand leaves water for recovery.

BK 24. Shane approaching camera as right hand has begun pull.

BK 25. Elbow is bent for downward thrust.

BK 26. Right hand pushes as left arm reaches up, about to enter water.

BK 27. Left arm enters water, little finger first.

BK 28. Note the "pigeon-toed" kick.

TURNING

The rules for backstroke swimming say that a swimmer must be on his back during the whole of the swimming part of the race. At the turn, he must touch with one hand while on his back, but in doing his turn he may alter position. After touching the wall, he tucks his legs up so that his knees are well bent and are out of the water. Then, with arms and head below the water, he turns slightly on his side, and with a rapid swivelling movement changes his direction. While still close to the wall, he pushes out with his feet, with knees well bent, and goes into a submerged glide with arms outstretched and legs straightening out for streamlining.

Beginners usually dislike backstroke thoroughly after they have had their first bumped head on the wall—and thereafter they spend most of the lap looking over their shoulders to see when the wall is coming up. Gay little flags at each end of the pool (stretched across the pool like bunting) are designed to avoid these mishaps, and are the equivalent of the markings on the bottom of the pool for the freestylers. Even small children can learn

BK 29. In the backstroke, there is always the danger of hitting the wall with your head instead of your hand. Flags across the pool ends help avoid this.

BK 30. Here is how a backstroke race starts—the swimmers are already in the water.

to count their strokes from the flags, and this eliminates anxiety about being hurt.

BACKSTROKE START

This is the only stroke which starts without a dive. The swimmer begins in the water, facing the starting end, grasping the grip-bar which is set into the blocks, body in a tense, crouching position, knees up under the chin, feet resting on the wall, and below the surface of the water. On "Go" the swimmer sends himself forcefully backwards over the water, flinging arms outwards (not above his head) as he pushes off the wall.

He takes a deep breath just before falling into the water. As he submerges shallowly, he stretches out his body to get the benefit of underwater glide before he begins his arm stroke.

7. Training

The most talented swimmer will never be a successful competitor without training. However, a talented youngster finds so much sheer pleasure from being in the water, that this pleasure will carry him over much of the hard work required to make him successful.

Shane's individual pattern of training within the framework of Forbes Carlile's swimming squad is the programme I know best.

The Carlile Swim School consists of four indoor centres plus the Ryde Outdoor Centre in summer. There are 50 staff employees, and they range from teachers of beginners (Learn-to-Swim), through elementary instructors to coaches of more advanced groups. The organization has had Olympic representatives on every Australian team since London in 1948. Shane is the 8th world-record holder to come out of the squad.

Although Australians regard Carlile's organization as one of the country's élite, the conditions under which he and his staff work and his swimmers train are far from ideal. A completely private enterprise which relies only on fees from students, it receives no governmental subsidy or club fee; neither do the swimmers' parents get a tax deduction for their fees paid. The pool facilities are costly to hire: the outdoor pool is not heated and the indoor pools, particularly Pymble, become very crowded in cold weather. On occasions there are as many as 20 swimmers in one lane of this 6-lane 25-metre pool! Obviously this presents difficulties of supervision and behaviour to say nothing of the difficulty of swimming good strokes (especially butterfly). There are three coaches working simultaneously with different ability-level groups for varying lengths of sessions.

In other areas, Australian swimmers train in open pools exposed to chilling winds so that their sessions are a real hardship. Shane's group is considered fortunate to have the facility of the Pymble Indoor Pool available to them. By comparison with American and European pools it is very substandard indeed.

The squad swims in a pool set up with lane-ropes, and each lane contains swimmers of roughly equal ability, so that the programme can be carried out without the slow ones being overtaken, or the little ones being swum over and nearly drowned!

The programme is chalked on a blackboard—not the whole day's or week's at once, but it is gradually written up as each distance is completed. The coach supervises, corrects stroke errors, encourages (and sometimes has to bully) the swimmers through their planned programme.

Shane personally enjoys most of the programmes. She likes training to have a change of pace, with some swimming done slowly, with thoughtful concentration

In swimming-training at Ryde open-air pool in Sydney, Coach Forbes Carlile is supervising correcting stroke errors and putting his swimmers through the planned programme.

on correct stroking, some done with about 80 per cent effort, and a series of timed laps in which she strives to swim each one faster than the one before. (She has a real aversion to being asked to swim three 1500's! The length of time required for these swims allows boredom to set in, concentration to wander, and enthusiasm to flag.) She prefers a pattern of varied strokes and distances broken by some verbal exchange with the coach and the opportunity for a little conversation with other swimmers as they wait for their next instructions.

She particularly enjoys the times when repeat swims are timed, and names and times are chalked up. Competitive feeling then runs high as each swimmer tries to improve on each subsequent time, and compares himself against his training mates. Sometimes these repeats can get pretty fast, and sometimes the swimmer can't finish one—so "C.O." (for "Chickened Out") appears on the blackboard instead of a time!

Carlile sets his pattern of training for his advanced swimmers over a week. With 40 miles the standard, each swimmer should achieve a certain number of miles with each stroke and a certain distance of kicking (legs only) and pulling (arms only).

Of equal importance to the number of miles swum in a week are the number of sessions. Carlile says that there is more value in swimming 10 sessions of 3 miles each, than 5 sessions of 6 miles each, because the swimmer is in a routine of training, he keeps in frequent touch with the water, and he doesn't suffer exhaustion.

Here is a sample of one week's session which Shane followed during March, 1972. These programmes were carried out at the end of the Australian summer season of swimming—after the major Championships, and just prior to the series of school championships. (There are three carnivals, roughly one week apart.)

SAMPLE TRAINING PROGRAMMES:

SUNDAY 6:00–8:00 a.m. 50-metre Pool
400m Freestyle Warm-up
800m Freestyle
16 × 100m Freestyle (every 1 min 45 sec)
800m Backstroke
8 × 50m Backstroke (every 60 sec)
200m Butterfly
6 × 100m Butterfly
400m Breaststroke
8 × 50m in Medley order (Butterfly, Backstroke, Breaststroke, Freestyle)   ......3½ miles

MONDAY 4:00–6:00 p.m. 25-metre Pool Indoors
800m Freestyle Warm-up
4 × 400m Freestyle (every 5 min 15 sec)
(Times: 4:45, 4:40, 4:30, 4:30)
2 × 200m Backstroke (every 2 min 45 sec)
(2:40, 2:35, "Chickened Out," 2:40)
400m Breaststroke Kicking on back
800m Breaststroke
8 × 100m Freestyle (every 2 min) (Average 63 sec)
4 × 100m Medley (every 2 min) (All 1:13)
16 × 25m Freestyle (every 30 sec)
16 × 25m Butterfly   ......4 miles

TUESDAY 5:15–7:00 a.m. 25-metre Pool Indoors
800m Freestyle Warm-up
8 × 100m Backstroke (every 2 min) (Average 1:18)
4 × 800m Freestyle (every 12 min)
(9:06, 9:07, 9:03, 8:54)
4 × 100m Medley (every 2 min)
400m Breaststroke
8 × 50m Butterfly   ......3¾ miles

TUESDAY 4:00–6:00 p.m. 25-metre Pool Indoors
800m Freestyle Warm-up
8 × 100m Butterfly (every 2 min) (Average 1:13)
400m Freestyle (4:33)
8 × 200m Freestyle (every 2 min 45 sec) (Average 2:24)
400m Breaststroke Kicking on back
16 × 50m Backstroke (every 50 sec)
16 × 25m Freestyle (every 45 sec—at maximum effort)
...... 4 miles

WEDNESDAY 9:30–3:30
Turramurra High School Carnival
No warm-up, no heats. Four final swims. 55-yd Pool
200m Individual Medley (2 min 28.0 sec)
200m Freestyle (2 min 09.8 sec)
100m Butterfly (1 min 09.2 sec)
100m Freestyle (59.2 sec)

THURSDAY 5:15–7:00 a.m. 25-metre Pool Indoors
800m Freestyle Warm-up
12 × 200m Freestyle (average 2 min 15 sec)
200m Freestyle Kicking
200m Backstroke (Broken by 5 sec rest at each end)
800m Medley
200m Breaststroke Kicking
400m Breaststroke Pulling
2 × 100m Breaststroke (every 2 min) (1:30, 1:19.7)
16 × 25m Butterfly (every 30 sec)
...... 3½ miles

THURSDAY 4:00–6:00 p.m. 25-metre Pool Indoors
800m Warm-up
16 × 100m Freestyle (every 1 min 30 sec)
(Average 65 sec)
16 × 50m Backstroke
200m Breaststroke Kicking
200m Breaststroke Pulling

800m Breaststroke
16 × 25m Butterfly
32 × 25m Freestyle
4 × 100m Medley (Average 1 min 13 sec)

. . . . . . 3¾ miles

FRIDAY 5:15–7:00 a.m. 25-metre Pool Indoors
800m Warm-up
16 × 50m Individual Medley Order
6 × 400m Freestyle (every 6 min)
(Last 3–4:40, 4:35, 4:28)
16 × 25m Freestyle (every 30 sec)
4 × 100m Butterfly (every 2 min)
8 × 25m Butterfly
8 × 24m Backstroke
400m Breaststroke

. . . . . . 3½ miles

SATURDAY 6:00–7:00 a.m. 50-metre Pool
400m Warm-up
800m Freestyle
2 × 400m Freestyle
4 × 100m Backstroke
400m Breaststroke
8 × 50m Butterfly

. . . . . . 2 miles

SATURDAY 1:30–3:30 p.m. 25-metre Pool Indoors
400m Freestyle Warm-up
800m Freestyle
5 × 400m Freestyle (every 5 min 30 sec)
8 × 100m Backstroke (every 1 min 45 sec)
4 × 50m Backstroke
8 × 100m Butterfly (every 2 min)
4 × 50m Butterfly
400m Breaststroke
8 × 50m Breaststroke

. . . . . . 3¾ miles

After the Easter recess, the winter programme in Australia begins, and sessions are longer in the mornings. Swimming from 4:45 a.m. to 7:00 a.m., the distance covered is around 5 miles.

STATISTICS OF SHANE'S TRAINING AND RACE RESULTS

June, 1970–March, 1971

Mid-June, 1970–Sept. 30, 1970
332 miles in 15 weeks
Average approximately 22 miles weekly
Normal training week—8 sessions
Longest mileage in one week—38 miles
Longest mileage in one session—4 miles

Sickness: One week of influenza

Racing:
(1) New South Wales Shortcourse (25-metre) Indoor Winter Championships, Sydney, August, 1970
100m Freestyle—1 min 00.9 sec
200m Freestyle—2 min 10.7 sec
400m Freestyle—4 min 33.4 sec
200m Individual Medley—2 min 32.0 sec
100m Backstroke—1 min 13.2 sec
100m Breaststroke—1 min 23.2 sec
100m Butterfly—1 min 10.0 sec

(2) Australian Winter Nationals Long Course (50-metre) Scarborough, Queensland, August, 1970
100m Freestyle—1 min 02.3 sec
200m Freestyle—2 min 17.2 sec
400m Freestyle—4 min 39.5 sec
200m Individual Medley—2 min 33.3 sec

Oct. 1, 1970–March 31, 1971
 779 miles in 26 weeks
 Average approximately 29 miles per week
 Normal training week—9 sessions
 Longest mileage in one week—42 miles
 Longest mileage in one session—5 miles

Sickness: Sore throat, 1 week

Racing:
(1) New South Wales State Championships (50-metre)
    Heffron Park Pool, Sydney, January, 1971
100m Freestyle—1 min 00.7 sec
200m Freestyle—2 min 11.1 sec
400m Freestyle—4 min 31.1 sec
800m Freestyle—9 min 24.2 sec
200m Individual Medley—2 min 33.3 sec

(2) Australian National Championships (50-metre),
    Hobart, Tasmania, February, 1971
100m Freestyle—1 min 00.3 sec
200m Freestyle—2 min 07.8 sec
400m Freestyle—4 min 26.2 sec
200m Individual Medley—2 min 29.2 sec

(3) Girls' Secondary School Swimming Carnival (50-
    metre), North Sydney, March, 1971
100m Freestyle—59.7 sec
200m Individual Medley—2 min 32.8 sec
200m Freestyle—2 min 10.6 sec

April 1, 1971–Sept. 30, 1971
 736 miles in 26 weeks
 Average approximately 28 miles per week
 Normal training week (when at home)—10 sessions
 Longest mileage in one week—45 miles
 Longest mileage in one session—6 miles (once only!)

Sickness: Nil

Absences from Regular Training:
  4 weeks, April–May, 1971 (European tour)
  1 week, California, July
  1 week holiday, September

Racing:
(1a) Crystal Palace, London (50-metre) April–May
100m Freestyle—58.9 sec
200m Freestyle—2 min 06.5 sec

(1b) Bonn, Germany (25-metre) May, 1971
100m Freestyle—58.1 sec
400m Freestyle—4 min 16.0 sec

(2) Santa Clara, California (50-metre) July, 1971
100m Freestyle—59.2 sec
200m Freestyle—2 min 06.61 sec
400m Freestyle—4 min 21.23 sec
800m Freestyle—9 min 03.87 sec

(3) Australian National Winter Championships, Valley
  Pool (50-metre), Brisbane, August, 1971
  100m Freestyle—1 min 00.2 sec
  200m Freestyle—2 min 11.2 sec
  400m Freestyle—4 min 23.8 sec
  800m Freestyle—9 min 03.2 sec
1500m Freestyle—17 min 19.4 sec

Oct. 1, 1971–March 31, 1972
  698 miles in 26 weeks
  Average approximately 27 miles per week
  Normal training week—9 sessions
  Longest mileage in one week—46 miles
  Longest mileage in one session—4½ miles

Sickness:
1 week influenza, Oct. 1971
1 week gastroenteritis, Feb. 1972

School Examinations: November

Racing:
(1) "Top Level" Meets Weekly (50-metre)
  200m Freestyle—2 min 05.8 sec Nov.
  800m Freestyle—8 min 58.1 sec Nov.
1500m Freestyle—17 min 00.6 sec Dec.

(2) New South Wales State Championships (50-metre),
    January, 1972
100m Freestyle—58.5 sec
200m Individual Medley—2 min 24.4 sec
400m Individual Medley—5 min 07.4 sec
100m Butterfly—1 min 05.1 sec

(3) Australian National Championships, Valley Pool
    (50-metre), Brisbane, Feb. 1972
100m Freestyle—1 min 00.2 sec
200m Freestyle—2 min 06.3 sec
400m Freestyle—4 min 22.8 sec
800m Freestyle—9 min 01.8 sec

(4) New Zealand Nationals (50-metre), Dunedin, Feb.
    1972
100m Freestyle—59.7 sec
200m Freestyle—2 min 07.7 sec

(5) New South Wales Secondary Schools Carnival,
    North Sydney Pool (50-metre) March, 1972
100m Freestyle—1 min 00.8 sec
200m Freestyle—2 min 08.3 sec
200m Individual Medley—2 min 28.6 sec

Best times in training since April 1971 (25-metre pool)
        25m.... 12.2 sec (dive)
        50m.... 27.4 sec (dive)
        100m.... 57.4 sec (dive)
        200m.... 2 min 04 sec (push off)
        400m.... 4 min 12 sec (push off)
        800m.... 8 min 52 sec (push off)
        1500m.... 16 min 53.4 sec (push off)
        2000m.... 23 min 17 sec (push off)
        3000m.... 35 min 09 sec (push off)
        5000m.... 60 min 35 sec (Swimathon, Ryde 50m)

SHANE'S PERSONAL ARRANGEMENTS FOR TRAINING

Time has to be very carefully used, especially on the days when Shane swims both in the morning and in the evening. There is no time available then for anything other than the essentials. This of itself is very satisfying— and in a sense amounts to "living each day as if it's your last." The non-essentials that are eliminated are valued tremendously when there is time for them. Shane therefore has the double advantage of learning to do something very well and enjoying the simple things of life with deep gratitude and pleasure because they are not commonplace for her. Such little experiences may be staying up until 10:30 at night to watch a movie on TV, going to a church fete, or watching her younger sisters' netball matches.

She has also learned to think ahead of the current activity so that she is rarely caught without the correct equipment for school. On the occasions when she is not completely ready herself, she gets willing help from the rest of the family simply because they are so infrequently "put upon."

The following list is her own routine for double-session swimming days.

PRACTICAL ARRANGEMENTS FOR TRAINING

Night Before:
1. Pack school bag.
2. Check on school clothes. Clean shoes.
3. Mix container of liquid food.
4. Have a dog biscuit available.
5. Set alarm for 4:20 a.m.

Morning:
1. Take heart rate (count pulse throbs for 30 sec; double this for H.R. per min).
2. Make bed.
3. Quiet dog with biscuit.
4. Drive with coach or parent to pool by 4:45, and swim under supervision until 7:00 a.m.
5. Home with father for breakfast, leave on school bus at 8:00 a.m.

School Day:
1. 30 mins before classes to read the newspapers in school library, or catch up on an assignment.
2. 30 mins free after eating lunch for any neglected preparation or reading in the library.
3. Home by 3:30 p.m. on the school bus.
4. If training in afternoon—snack of liquid food, or coffee and cookies.
5. Drive (with mother or friend) to pool by 4:00 p.m.
6. Swim until 6:00 p.m.

Evening:
1. Home by 6:30 p.m.
2. Dinner with family (TV and conversation).
3. Study for one hour.
4. To bed by 8:00 p.m. after making arrangements for morning.

Week-ends: Saturday
1. Training 6:00–7:30 a.m.
2. Club races 7:30–10:00 a.m.
3. Rest of morning in home chores—e.g., cleaning room, ironing, baking, helping to prepare lunch.

4. Afternoon free for visiting, movies, sailing, etc. Usually some study included. A sleep in afternoon if tired.

Sunday's programme is flexible—but during the week-end Shane usually manages about 6–8 hours of school work. Assignments at her school are planned so that a week-end intervenes between the setting and handing-in date.

Shane's pattern of training has changed over the months. For April and May of '72 she had 7 early morning sessions and 3 only for the afternoons, allowing more study time. She swam 40 miles in these 10 sessions.

LOG BOOK

Keeping a log book, as the ship's pilot keeps his log, was a new experience for Shane when she joined the Carlile organization. She fills in the entries for each day's training while waiting for dinner to be served, or just before going to bed. The value of a log book lies primarily in the coach's knowing exactly how his training programme is working out for each individual swimmer. Shane has aimed at honesty; filling in longer distances than she has actually swum is pointless to her. Subjective comments about the way she feels (aches, pains, tiredness, emotional "flatness," happiness and enthusiasm) together with the objective evidence of heart-rate, hours of sleep, and times done in training are all useful pieces of information for a swimmer in learning about himself or herself.

Shane has found from the accounts in her log book that a consistent routine of school and swimming-training and regular hours of sleep have resulted in good swimming times. Her performances have been upset by both late nights and the occasional very long (6 miles) of swimming-training. Particularly good times have followed when her heart rate was very low; she knows then that she is very fit, and becomes confident of expecting her best in physical performance.

The coach's comment gives the swimmer something more to strive for, or gives encouraging explanations for problem situations.

Here is a sample of a page from Shane's log book.

PAGE FROM SHANE'S LOG BOOK

Pymble Indoor Pool (25m) Week Number 12 Commencing on Sunday 20.6.71	Weight 58 kgs (131 lbs) (in swimsuit, weekly)	Height 5'8" (Barefoot, weekly)

Day		Miles Actually Swum	Early Morning Heart Count (mins)	Sleep hours	Study & Home-Work. hours	General Diary Details of training, best times for repeats. Race results, health, how you feel, stroke corrections to remember, exam results, important happenings, immediate & future, goals, why <u>full</u> training not done (if it is not).
SUN	am	5		8½		Didn't train very well this morning. Couldn't get on top of the water. Arms pretty sore and I'm tired. Winter Time Trials - in afternoon -100m FS 60.8, 200 BS 2.56.6(best), 400 IM 5m17.6 (OK).
	pm	1				
MON	am	3½		9½	1½	Felt horrible this morning - couldn't be bothered. Much better this afternoon though. 400 FS 4.20, 200 Fly 2.36, 50 Fly 34.
	pm	3¾				
TUES	am		40	8½	½	Arms, shoulders and hips sore from shotput and hurdles at school. But felt good in water - could feel the strength of the water against me. 800 FS 8.52 (It's true)
	pm	5				
WED	am	4¼		10	1	Didn't feel very good today - OK though. Stroke in FS not right?? 400 FS 4.19.2.
	pm	4½				
THUR	am			9	½	Had all day off swimming. Went to a Reception which the Prime Minister attended. Karen Moras and I were presented with watches by Mrs Sonia McMahon - a fantastic experience!
	pm					
FRI	am	3½		9	¾	(Doing a lot of work at school before classes and at lunchtime). Felt pretty good today. Went to Orthodontist in pm - so only short session. 25 FS 12.8.
	pm	1½				
SAT	am	5¼		8½		Felt pretty good this morning. Went out with John and his family all day. 200 FS 2.05, 100 BK 1.18, 1500 FS 18.25.
	pm					

Weekly Total (miles)	37¼	Coach's Comments Really good swimming on Sunday, Shane - looks as though you are finding your form again. I feel you could benefit considerably from regular (every day) dynastatic. Tom.	Parents Comment & Requests.
Progressive Total for Season	350½		

TAPERING OR PEAKING

There is a change of emphasis in training when a swimmer is planning to taper for championship events. Shane has never really peaked in the American sense (i.e., swum so hard in training over three months that her muscles have ached badly and her times have been extremely slow, then rested and swum well at a championship). Swimming the whole year round, she has been able to come up with world record swims in January, April, July, November and December. She has done this by avoiding extremes of fatigue and resting although there has been some moderation in the pattern of her training prior to championships.

The whole physical process of training for competition can be compared with the operation of a mechanical toy—training is winding it up, tapering is holding the springs in readiness, and racing is letting the mechanism go. Many coaches wish that training swimmers were as simple as this, depending only on mechanical or physical processes!

The tapering on Shane's squad is very individual, and is worked out by the coach according to each one's needs. Some swimmers who have trained for many years find that their bodies are so conditioned to long distances in training that they need to keep swimming distance right up to championship time in order to keep in touch with the water, and to keep their speed up. Some who have had little background of training may need a week of minimum swimming so that their muscles adjust to feeling relaxed and comfortable and ready to swim fast. These swimmers are only in the process of building up condition.

Shane now likes her tapering period to be about 7–10 days of slackening off the hard training, but still doing some shorter-distance swimming. She also enjoys the days of "sharpening up" when she practises starts, turns and finishes, and short sprints are timed. During this tapering period, parents often find that their swimmers are so full of unexpended vitality that they are mischievous, cheeky, and altogether a little larger than life! There is often an outbreak of rough-house play, demand for picnics, displays of strength, or furniture-moving routines. If you can anticipate it, this is a good time for parents to arrange to have the garage or attic thoroughly cleaned, and gardens re-planned, in order to skim off excess energy!

Once the championships start, all the efforts are channelled into racing.

EXERCISES

Without realizing it, Shane was probably doing a considerable amount of swimming-exercising when she was a small child in Fiji. Daily she swung from ropes and trapezes rigged up in massive mango trees. She and her friends spent hours climbing up and down swinging ladders to the tree houses they constructed. She could "chin the bar" before she was 8 years old.

The Nadi Airport School also had a strong emphasis on sport and physical fitness due to the influence of the Headmaster, Ron Bruce. The 100-student school had first-class climbing frames and the school's walls were used for paddle tennis and other ball games. Folk dancing was regarded as too "sissy" by both boys and girls, so basketball, softball, captain-ball, tunnel-ball, tumbling and athletics took over instead. Visiting school teams competed on frequent occasions and this sharpened the practices.

Shane's early years were unusually physically active. On visits to her grandparents in Sydney she felt very restricted by the suburban house as she had to be stopped from swinging on door-lintels and somer-saulting over chairs. She really earned Grandfather's nickname for her of "Jumping Bean." Even in sleep, her muscles twitched.

Channelling all this activity into swimming-training certainly tamed Shane and made her more able to accept the restriction of a regular school.

Shane was first encouraged to use a pulling machine to supplement her light winter training, by Bruce McDonald. Bruce was Shane's coach during the years 1967–1968 when we lived in Epping (a suburb of the northern districts of Sydney) and Shane was a member of the Eastwood-Epping Amateur Swimming Club. The machine works on the resistance principle—by making adjustments, resistance can be increased or decreased.

When swimming twice a day, Shane hasn't felt so much need to use the exerciser, and in fact is hard-pressed to find time for even 5 minutes of pulling. If she swims only once, she usually tries to do at least 10 minutes, and her coach would have her do more. Shane often needs to be reminded to do the exercises, but she is always glad when she has done them as she feels the groups of muscles in shoulders and upper arms flexing as she does a simulated freestyle pull. She feels certain that it does help her stroking and her strength.

The other use for this exerciser is in making the muscles warm and limbered up for racing. If there is no time for a warm-up swim, or if there is a long wait between events, using the exerciser is very helpful.

Some swimmers do a lot of dry-land exercises and weight-lifting; Shane only does a few sit-ups to strengthen abdominal muscles, and a few shoulder and wrist flexibility movements.

MENTAL ATTITUDE TO TRAINING

Any reasonably perceptive pool-side observer will notice that swimmers vary considerably in their mental attitudes to swimming-training, and that these attitudes condition behaviour.

Most swimmers begin training because someone has

Leg pull with the exerciser.

The exerciser attached to the house is fine for practising the backstroke pull.

(Right) The exerciser improves arm strokes.

(Below) Freestyle pull with the exerciser.

told them that they are "good" and have "swimming potential." Parents, flattered, feeling a measure of pride in having produced a youngster of promise, decide that they will give their child an opportunity to realize his potential.

Next, let us assume that the youngster has the physical capacity to undertake training and notice that the intangibles of the situation take on interesting patterns.

The child of privilege sometimes lacks the goading incentive that the "battler's" kid has—the latter knows that without some achievement in swimming he may be without recognition, and he also knows he has more to gain through swimming success than his family can ever give him.

The underprivileged youngster's parents tend therefore to force him into training for the sake of the rewards he may get directly (and they get vicariously) out of swimming. Rewards vary from popularity at school, to trophies at club meets (some clubs give very generous trophies), and most important of all, travel within the country or overseas with a team. Travel is a very expensive commodity for Australians, whose country is so far from the other English-speaking ones, so this incentive is highly regarded and competition for inclusion in a team is fierce.

Those children of all economic groups who have become accustomed to their demands being met rather readily find that the long hours of "adapting the body to take stress" (i.e., hours of swimming-training) make him wonder why the results are so slow to show. Impatient for quick success, he either swims too fast to get through the session rapidly and show how "good" he is, or he will only half listen to the description of the stroke and hurry on to the practice without really fully comprehending the basics. Another group of swimmers could be called the "Cheaters." They think that they are doing swimming-training, but they are really

Helping at the pool is expected of everyone, world champion or beginner. Here Shane is putting away the kicking boards at Ryde Pool, under Coach Carlile's direction.

wasting their time, their parents' money, and the coach's patience. They swim reasonably consistently if they are under close scrutiny, but if the coach is called away they start "walking," pulling on the ropes, submerging and changing direction so that they do only half a lap. (Almost every swimmer at some time during months of training would be "guilty" of some of these tricks!) They feel tired and cannot take the full programme, they feel rebellious at the requirement for disciplined effort, or perhaps they wonder at times what they are doing in swimming-training at all.

When this behaviour is rare or only occasional, tiredness, health factors, or some temporary psychological reason can usually be blamed, but if it is almost perpetual, it indicates a much deeper dissatisfaction, and parents and swimmer would do well to examine their motives for participating at all. Swimmers of this type, especially if they are very talented "naturals" drive coaches to angry frustration and cause very real disruption to the other swimmers' training. Somewhere along the line the "cheating" swimmer has failed to identify himself as a swimmer in search of excellence; he is in swimming-training for some reason, but certainly not for the only really valid one, of doing it because he alone wants to, and because he is aiming at achieving personal satisfaction.

The constant cheater's parents would do better to encourage him to swim for fun and fitness, cutting down sessions to a minimum, and working on a more comfortable programme without feeling guilty about it.

The Australian swimming scene contains very few real masochists—the pain-seekers who drive themselves to the very limit of their physical capacity for endurance, and feel real pleasure when they are in pain. Some do achieve success, but at what a price! The sport of swimming cannot be blamed for their personality problems.

Occasionally a squad will contain fiercely competitive swimmers. These boys and girls are aggressively determined to make it into championship class, and will use very trick in training to promote themselves and spoil the other swimmers' chances. Swimmers like this cannot lose gracefully; their excuses come thick and fast. Their measure of success is in having beaten an enemy, not in having done their personal best. They deliberately unsettle other competitors before races, and cause interference in training schedules. At face value, their dedication to determined effort looks admirable; on closer inspection, it is twisted and self-destroying. Far from being an asset to a coach, they are an embarrassment, as they are too aggressively self-seeking, and so undermine the solidarity of the training squad as a co-operative group. For all their unpleasantness they sometimes earn a grudging sympathy for their loneliness, because they never really "belong" to the group.

Every person in swimming-training brings to it his own mental attitude coloured by experience, hurts and triumphs, by recognition in his peer group, pride of parents, and the thrusts of ambition from inside or outside himself.

SOME SOCIAL DYNAMICS OF SWIMMING-TRAINING

Every teen-ager needs to belong to some group. Belonging, conforming within the group, testing himself out against the others, learning about independence within the security of the group, understanding the differences of the sexes are all matters of supreme importance to a teen-ager.

A swimming squad provides an excellent framework for all these needs. In some ways a squad is similar to attending a special class at school, except that the attendance is voluntary, and the "examinations" are optional. Swimmers get very close to each other, both in the physical and the psychological sense. They are in a situation where superficialities cease to be relevant, and only the real person and his swimming ability matters.

As in any group, the dynamics are interesting. Stratified groups develop, usually based on swimming performance; leaders emerge; cliques and subgroups exist.

The leader is frequently prepared to take on the onus of swimming first in a line of swimmers. This means he has to be sure he can maintain his lead and not lose face by being overtaken. He will run the risk of being criticized by the others if he does not keep an even pace and speed to suit their needs, and he is constantly being challenged by new would-be leaders.

Sub-groups consist of close friends, weaker or lazy swimmers, groups of adolescent boys trying to show off their emergent manhood for the admiration of the girls, groups of girls who feel insecure about being near to the boys, etc. These little sub-groups are constantly re-forming and are generally in a state of flux.

An established squad with the same membership

for a lengthy period can undergo upheaval or even disintegration if a newcomer of outstanding potential arrives. The group tends to tighten its structure against the outsider and show its disapproval of change by over-reacting in training, or disobeying the coach's instructions. As the coach normally watches a new swimmer pretty closely, the squad's misbehaviour is intended to direct the coach's attention back to them, away from the new swimmer!

The earlier, well-understood social order of the swimmers will necessarily be forced into a rearrangement if the newcomer challenges the leaders in swimming performance. As the newcomer takes up his position there has to be a down-grading of everyone weaker than he, and this naturally brings resentment and anger from those who are supplanted. Charges of "favouritism" are levelled at the coach, parents become involved, and small incidents are taken out of context and blown up out of all proportion in dressing-room gossip.

At meets, the old group will suddenly become a cheer squad for the old leaders, and will remain silent if the newcomer wins.

If the new swimmer continues to improve and goes on to beat the previous champion, it is predictable that the ousted champion will either retire from the sport, or change squads. (Displaced champions then become the unsettling influence in their new squad.) Journalists unwittingly aggravate situations like this when they build up the new champion at the expense of the old one. Teen-agers are notoriously thin-skinned where the printed word is concerned, and extensive confidence-building is needed to overcome the hurt of defeat, so that they can present themselves bravely for the next competition.

Not all group activity is destructive or exclusive. By being cohesive against the newcomers, the "establishment" strengthens itself, however damaging this may be to the newcomer. More important, it is almost impossible for a swimmer to carry out a programme of 4 miles of varied training completely alone—yet in a squad he can do it at every session! The reason seems to be group participation. The unspoken thought "if he can do it, so can I" is a constant incentive. And the fact is that a 800m lone swim is disheartening, while swimming the same distance when the goal is to keep one's hands close to the other swimmer's feet is easier to accept.

There is a point at which most swimmers in a squad "use" each other. As long as this is reasonably reciprocal, no one minds. However, there are times when the lane-leader wants a rest from his chore of pace-setting, and he can become resentful of his companions and his coach if he is forced to continue. Muttered complaints about being "used as the work-horse for the squad" can grow into unpleasantly paranoid attitudes. The wise coach seeing this development usually thanks the leader for doing his share, but says "now it's so-and-so's turn."

TIREDNESS

Training would be meaningless if it did not demand a physical effort which ended in genuine bodily weariness. A good meal and a good night's sleep should overcome this, although there may be a residual muscle-soreness which lasts either until more training has caused adaptation in the muscle, or resting has eased it. Shane is less bothered with this soreness than she was when she first began serious training, and felt she had to push herself to reach the standard the others had already achieved. However, there are still times when she experiences a tight trapezius muscle (in the shoulder) or some soreness in the triceps (upper arm). She finds some easing of this by taking hot showers, using an infra-red lamp, or motherly massage, which is more a gesture of sympathy than of therapy. If the soreness is persistent, she skips a training session or two, and works only on her pulling exerciser.

FUN AND GAMES

Not all swimming-training is serious drudgery. Young people manage to have fun whenever they are together in a group, and this is one of the things which keeps them in training. Talking between laps is frowned upon by the coach, yet he allows much of it because he knows it is a necessary diversion. Too much of it, and especially while the coach is talking, is plain rudeness and deserves censure. Some conversations manage to keep going for half an hour in snatched sentences between laps. During the laps the swimmers think up smart replies, and this also breaks the tedium of distances.

One game favoured by Shane's group is "dragging." This is done during fast swims, and the idea is to swim along as fast as possible, while keeping within the "wash" of the swimmer ahead in the lane. This creates large waves in the next lanes, but unruffled water for the swimmers within the "drag." Some surprisingly fast times result from this game.

One very warm and closely knit squad (at Woolooware) which Shane belonged to at the age of 10, followed a series of bizarre fashions. For weeks all the youngsters wore sun-glasses and "beanies" (woollen caps)—another time they all draped themselves with rugs so that the poolside looked like an Indian reservation. Group togetherness was very actively fostered by the coaches Harry Gibbons and his son John, as they felt they got more quality of work from the group when all were happy to be working together.

The Fortitude Club in Brisbane had a game of "Shark" which certainly hurried the line swimming along. This game consisted of swimming close enough to the one in front to take a bite at his toes! At the ends of the pool, while waiting for instructions, this squad also had the most dextrous water "squirters." Cupping their hands together and squirting water through narrow apertures, they had perfect aim and their distance was remarkable. Needless to say, this game was not actively encouraged by the coach, but it provided many an enjoyable interval for the swimmers.

This same squad often completed laps in amazing times by the co-operative device of pulling each other along—one swimmer going down the lane would take the hand of the swimmer coming towards him, and pull vigorously (in the Allemande fashion of square-dancing) so that each would get a good boost along. These harmless games made light work of training and served as comic relief from effort swimming.

Water Polo after the Sunday morning races was also a great source of fun. Dr. Van Opdenbosch, an Olympic Water Polo player, was the coach of the Fortitude Club—and under his exuberantly enthusiastic leadership, the Sunday morning games (which included the girls) were really riotous fun.

Brad Cooper, later to become world-record holder in the 400m and 800m freestyle, and Australian team member for the Olympics in Munich 1972, also belonged to this Fortitude squad at the same time as Shane was training in Brisbane with Gordon Petersen.

Bruce McDonald used the incentive of a "free go on the trampoline" both as a warm-up for the usually cold pool at Dence Park, Epping, or as a reward for good training effort. The trampoline in 1967 was not common equipment and the swimmers enjoyed both the novelty and the warming effect it produced.

Shane was tall but very slim without a good insulating layer of fat at this time, and the 62° water frequently turned her blue with cold. But after a good bounce on the trampoline she became rosy and exhilarated. She was never under any compulsion to "stay there and finish those laps" when the water was too cold for her.

Bruce McDonald had no intention of pushing her too hard as a young swimmer; he wanted to ensure that she stayed in swimming until she was fully grown and really strong. His predictions (when she was 10) of "world records before she turns 16" were never taken seriously by the family at that time, but looking back, it is interesting to recall that he felt she had exceptional ability at that early age. Shane was very fortunate to have been associated with this far-seeing man in those early stages of disciplined swimming-training.

While Shane recognizes the importance of the coach, she feels that the squad is of enormous value to her, too. She feels at ease with the other swimmers. Since fame has come her way she is often stared at or pointed at in public places, but at the pool, in her squad, she is just another swimmer who shares conditions with all the others. It is also a salutary experience for Shane to talk to the younger swimmers, and ask them about their "best times." She often finds that many of them are better than she could manage at their ages, and this leads Shane to take a larger perspective on record-breaking. She realizes that the new generation will always improve on the older one, and that her own records will be broken—and this gives her a mental cushioning against the time when she will be superseded.

8. Racing

Preparing for a race is rather like getting ready for an examination. You know you have studied hard, but on the actual day you may not feel too well, or something occurs which influences how you will write the answers. The same thing happens in swimming. The race effort can be upset for many reasons: a poor night's sleep, maybe due to the neighbours having a party, or perhaps over-excitement, an ordinary cold, or unpleasant weather—too cold or too hot. Maybe you have stiff muscles in unexpected places because the Physical Education teacher has given you a hard work-out. There are so many variables; not all can be controlled, but you must do your best to handle and anticipate as many as possible.

SHANE'S RACE DAY PLAN

First, a good night's sleep—10 hours if possible. Then, up in the morning about an hour and a half before leaving for the pool. A hot shower, and a breakfast fairly high in calories. Here are some example breakfasts:

1. Fruit juice, spaghetti or baked beans on toast. Tea or coffee.

2. Juice, stewed fruit in syrup served with the powdered form of a commercial liquid food.

3. Juice, fried rice, toast with honey. (The fried rice consists of finely cut bacon fried in a pan, scrambled egg added and cooked together, cold cooked rice added and heated through.)

Shane personally avoids milk and large steaks as she finds they take too long for her to digest. After breakfast, she gets her equipment ready for the day, and checks each item off her list. Doing it herself means that she knows exactly what she is taking with her.

1. One swimsuit for each event, and one for the warm-up.
2. Bathing cap.
3. Track suit and club T-shirt.
4. Two towels.
5. Pool shoes and socks (cold day). Rubber thongs (hot day).
6. Underclothes for wearing home.
7. Sleeping bag, scarf, woollen cap, sweater if cold.
8. Sun-hat and sun-glasses on hot days.
9. Exercising machine.
10. Containers of liquid food (2 or 3).
11. Pack of cards, book, paper and pen.

If Shane knows she has to stay at the pool over the lunch period, then she takes along something like chicken stew and rice in a wide-mouthed thermos flask. Orange juice and dried fruits are her favourite snacks at a race.

In Australia, championship meets are usually held at night (7 or 8 p.m.) with the heats (preliminaries) in the morning (9 a.m.). It is understood that swimmers arrive at the pool an hour earlier for a warm-up swim supervised by the coach—often a slow 800m followed by timed 100's or 50's.

WARMING UP

This short swim gets the muscles moving and flexible and in addition has value in being, in effect, a familiarization exercise. Shane always tries to concentrate on her dives, strokes and turns. She pays special attention to the painted markings on the bottom of the pool as they help her to judge when she should do her tumble turn. For instance, at one pool she knows that she can do $2\frac{1}{2}$ strokes of freestyle after passing over the end of the line before flipping over and pushing off the wall with her feet. Swimmers know that bad judgment can give you a very sore pair of heels if the turn is too late; and

Shane (with Brad Cooper) has already warmed up and is now trying to keep her muscles warm before racing.

they get no push-off if they turn too early and only lightly brush the wall. Worst of all, they are disqualified if they fail to touch the wall altogether!

After the warm-up, Shane tries to have a hot shower, but, regrettably, pools do not always have this facility. If the weather is cold, the next problem is to keep her muscles warm until it is time to swim. Getting into a dry swimsuit, track suit, socks, and into the sleeping bag is a good idea if there is a long time to wait. About 15 minutes before being called for the race, Shane often does some pulling work on the exerciser. On the occasion of her world-record swim in the 200m freestyle (2 min 5.8 sec) she arrived too late at the pool for a warm-up swim, and she only used her little machine to warm-up.

RACING INSTRUCTIONS

Some coaches, especially those with small squads, like to give their swimmers detailed instructions for a particular race, just before it is swum. Shane's coach for the years 1967–1968, Bruce McDonald, was one of these. A big man with an expansive personality, he used to get her into a quiet corner just prior to the race and tell her in conspiratorial manner how she was going to beat all the others! Shane was alert and receptive, and if she won the race she was quite sure that Bruce's strategy had worked for her.

What did he say? Something like this . . . "Now, Shane, this race is going to be yours if you follow my plan. Stand steadily on the block, and when the gun goes off, get a really strong, outstretched start. Settle down in your stroking for the first 25 metres, don't think about the others, just concentrate on how your stroke is working. Then over the next 25 metres swim a bit harder and go strongly into the turn. Get a good push-off, and put in the solid work on the way back, but make sure you have some reserve left for the finish. About 10 metres from the end, put everything out, and then old girl, swim straight through that wall!"

This of course is a perfect general description of how to swim a good race—and 11-year-old Shane felt certain that she had the most special, almost magical formula for winning that race! Bruce's manner of conveying very ordinary information was so intimate and secretive, that it created a tremendous bond of trust between herself and the coach.

Naturally, no one can win a race on last-minute instructions only. The preparation beforehand is what makes for a winner, and Bruce McDonald knew this very well. But he also knew that Shane was somewhat overawed by the confidence of the opposition swimmers of the Ryde club (coached by Forbes Carlile) and he gave her a dose of confidence to overcome her awe. Last-minute instructions like Bruce's are very positive thoughts to occupy the mind, and give a sense of assurance, and an easing of tension. There is no room for negative, self-defeating thoughts like "Will I last the distance?" or, "My arms are feeling weak, and my heart is bumping."

In a large squad, too many swimmers vie for the coach's attention, and he cannot afford to become too closely involved with one and ignore the others. But what is perhaps lost in the close coach–swimmer relationship is more than compensated for by sharing with others, and the assurance of knowing exactly what to do, as all the others are doing the same.

Forbes Carlile has to resort to almost weekly "bulletins" to get across special information to his squads because they train in different pools with several different coaches. Prior to competition he writes an excellent resumé of racing preparation; this bulletin travels the country widely—and is often used without acknowledgment to the author!

PSYCHING UP

Beforehand, if the race is for "fun," Shane likes to be with young friends, playing cards, exchanging jokes and gossiping. If the race is an important one for her, then she is pretty unsociable. She tries to get her thoughts concentrated on what she is about to do. She

Shane is concentrating on a mental picture of how she will win her race, how she will pace it. At this point, no one can talk to her.

ignores people making light chatter, and is very easily irritated by people asking questions. Parents especially will offend her at this time if they ask—"Have you got your socks on?" or some other foolish irrelevancy. At this time she is thoroughly anti-social, completely unable to cheer up a friend who has had a disappointing swim, and barely polite to any breathless little autograph-hunter. She is totally involved in a mental picture of how she will swim the race, what effort she will put into each section of it, and how she will pace it.

MARSHALLING

Swimmers are called to the marshalling area about three races ahead of the one they are competing in. This gives the officials a chance to check their names and be certain that the listed swimmers are in fact going to swim. At this time, all the competitors are together in a situation which can feel threatening to the unconfident ones. In Australian swimming, there is very little attempt to psych-out each other, but even light talk or good-humoured teasing can appear deliberately provocative or unsettling to a highly keyed, emotional or sensitive competitor. If a swimmer knows he is susceptible to this, he would do best to sit quietly and

After being marshalled, Shane sits off by herself. Even light banter can upset her now.

Shane (middle) goes to the starting block as the 1500-meter freestyle in December, 1971, is about to begin. In this race she set a world record.

"tune out" of all the conversation, or occupy himself in doing some arm-winding exercises!

The marshal calls each swimmer to the blocks for the start of the race, and the check-starter double-checks names of the competitors. If it is a race of some importance, and is of spectator interest, then each swimmer is introduced as he mounts his block, and his achievements are mentioned briefly. Sometimes this is done by an announcer, and occasionally he makes a small error, inadvertently causing the swimmer untold embarrassment. Swimmers generally feel that this is the time they dislike most. Standing at the back of their blocks, being introduced, wishing the race would start, they find the waiting interminable.

STARTING

The starter says "Quiet for the start of the race," then "Take your marks." At this the swimmers move forward to the front edge of their blocks, curl their toes over the edge, and bend over, ready for a dive. Some swimmers like to start in a "grab" position—this means they simply hold onto the side of the block. Those with long arms

Shane waits for the gun. Bent almost double, her arms hanging down almost to her toes, she keeps hands and arms well relaxed.

and a tendency to overbalance, use this technique but it is not general in Australia.

Shane starts as described in the freestyle section. She waits for the gun by bending low, arms down, in front of her legs, hands and arms relaxed. On "GO" she shoots her arms backward rapidly with elbows bent, then outstretches them in front of her as she dives from the block. She gets tremendous thrust from her fast arm movement, and from the push off the block. From several photographs of racing starts, it would seem that she tends to fly higher than the others, but she certainly comes up out of the water slightly ahead. Her entry is shallow and forceful, and seems to stun her for a second! Her body is completely tensed and outstretched—notice her fingers in the photograph. Under the water she waits for the glide to carry her along. Then her head appears, and she starts her stroking.

Shane gets a tremendous thrust from shooting her arms backward and then rapidly forward in front of her as she dives from the block.

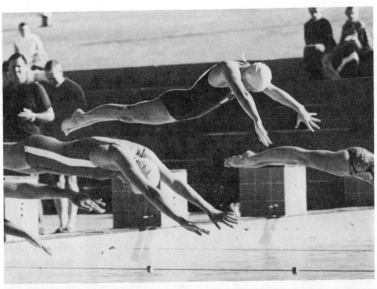

In this race Shane is far higher in the air than her rivals and her arms are not outstretched yet. The others will hit the water sooner, but Shane will be out farther.

RACING SWIMMER OR CLOCK?

Shane usually studies the names of the other competitors on the programme, and if she knows their ability then she has some idea of whether she will be swimming against them, or against the clock. As she has become a better swimmer, she has had to race against time, as she is the one the others are trying to beat! For the spectators, the most exciting races are those in which the competitors are evenly matched and each one uses his own method of racing—some will go hard early, others will save themselves for a final burst, and so on.

Sometimes, of course, a swimmer feels disappointed by the way he swam. He might have too much energy left over at the end of the race, energy he could well have used earlier. More often the inexperienced swimmer will "go out like a lion" and come home like the proverbial lamb! All his energy goes as he uses up too much oxygen too early in the race, instead of rationing the effort evenly.

Before a race, Shane usually studies the programme to see who her rivals will be.

Shane's legs are perfectly straight as she hits the water like an arrow.

In this orthodox dive, Shane is not flying as high as usual. Her entry is shallow but forceful. Her body is tensed and her fingers outstretched to their limit.

PACING A RACE

"Pace" is learnt over many miles of training. A swimmer learns to count the number of arm strokes needed to swim one length of the pool, and he soon finds that there is a different number for a fast swim than for a slow training swim, or for a distance swim. More than this, he learns from the sensation of the water's surge around him what a fast swim feels like. His body, too, has a different feeling when it is being pushed to the effort his mind wants it to undertake. Learning pace, however, is not sheer rote application of repetitive training, but an intelligent and reflective consideration of the responses of the body and the water's reaction to his movement through it. These conclusions are stored in memory. The feeling can be recaptured in training practice and gradually the method can become so automatic that he can swim consistently fast times. Coach or even parents can help in recall by asking their swimmer simple questions like "How did you feel in that race when you did such a good time? What were you doing that made everything work so well for you?"

Shane tries to swim her races as evenly as possible, so that each lap is approximately the same. In a race longer than the 100-metre, her first and last laps are usually the fastest. The first has the advantage of the dive and her own freshness, the last because she always plans to leave something for the finish of the race.

In the 100-metre swim, she uses bilateral breathing for most of the first 50 metres. Her stroke becomes progressively faster and stronger, and in the second 50 metres she breathes unilaterally as she increases her oxygen debt. For the last 3 or 4 metres she tries to put her head down and finish on one breath. The dilemma of whether to take another stroke or whether to stretch out for the finish is always there at the end of the race.

In sprints, Shane breathes bilaterally for the first half, then unilaterally as she speeds up. For the last few metres, she puts her head down and finishes in one breath.

Mostly, Shane stretches for the finish and says afterwards, "Maybe I should have taken another stroke!"

SPECTATORS

Another part of the race day is the spectator's contribution. Swimmers in a race give a performance, and they respond to the cheers and excitement of the onlookers. A good announcer can encourage a crowd to cheer on a possible record swim. The swimmer out front knows by the sounds around him if he is in sight of a record. This exciting knowledge which he shares with the spectators can often give him that little extra spur to put out an effort he didn't know he had! Brad Cooper, Karen Moras, Grahame Windeatt and Shane (all Australia's recent world-record holders) have commented on this.

Part of the crowd that came to the North Sydney pool in January, 1972 to see Shane try to break the 100-metre record.

Music is the other external stimulus which can help a swimmer. Shane particularly enjoys band music— strong beat and heavy rhythm, between her events. It relaxes unnecessary tension, yet gives her very pleasant stimulation.

END OF THE RACE

When the race is over, the swimmers must remain in the water until the officials have worked out times and places. The official then blows a whistle, and says "You may leave the water now." The timekeeper gives the competitor a card with his official time recorded on it, the swimmer collects his clothes or towels, and the next stop he makes should be with the coach for a short "Post Mortem" of the race. Talking to the coach soon after the race means being given valuable comments which may later slip from the coach's mind as he watches many subsequent races. Information like this should be remembered, the positive points used in later races, and the errors worked out in training.

Shane finishing the race that all Australia wanted to see—100 metres in 58.5 seconds, a new world record.

Shane learnt an important lesson when she was 12, and was "touched out" of a race by the outstanding young Queenslander, Helen Gray. In training, Shane had been used to gliding into the finish, and she automatically did this in the race when she and Helen were perfectly matched. Helen won the race on her last two strokes when she practically hurled herself to the finishing wall!

WINNING AND LOSING

Swimming is highly competitive. Frequently a race meet will have 40 entrants for one event, all of whom have "qualified," that is, reached a certain time standard for eligibility to participate. Qualifying in itself is a mark of achievement. Of the 40 entrants, 32 will be eliminated in the heats so that only 8 get to swim in the final. And of these 8, only 3 receive trophies—medals, ribbons, etc., and only the winner's time is mentioned in the local newspaper!

Yet the swimmer who was placed 35th may have

bettered his previous time by a large margin, and should be entitled to praise and encouragement from his coach and parents, whereas the winner may be genuinely disappointed because his apparently good time was below his personal "best." Satisfaction out of racing is always relative and highly individual.

Newcomers to a swimming meet may be pleasantly surprised to see little 8-year-olds solemnly shaking hands and offering congratulations to the one who has just beaten them—although they perhaps later run to Mum and have a surreptitious tear wiped away. The hand-shaking, however basically insincere, is a positive gesture and gives a youngster a momentary sense of generosity of spirit. It is also a practice at dealing graciously with a small slice of life's adversity! A simple phrase like, "You swam a good race, Fred," marks a young person as a champion in sportsmanship even if he never wins a medal.

Grahame Windeatt with aching sinuses swam as strongly as he was able, to push his teammate, Brad Cooper, to take his own 800m world record—and he congratulated Brad warmly afterwards. Karen Moras, on losing her 400m world record to Shane at Santa Clara made a real sportsman's comment—"If I had to lose, I'm glad it went to another Australian. I think Shane is fabulous."

"I swam the best I could today," is a champion's statement, one that is understood and appreciated by all other swimmers.

Of course, there will be "soul-searching" discussions after the race; lessons are learnt, new ideas are discussed for the next time. Sometimes swimmers who are good at a variety of strokes attempt too many events at a carnival. Then they find, when about to swim their favourite event, that their strength has been dissipated and the opposition is too strong. A large number of events may be a good idea if a swimmer is lacking experience in

Shane (lane 5) is beaten by Karen Moras in a 400-metre time trial before the European tour of May, 1971, begins.

racing (and therefore allowance should be made for poor times), but many events can be exhausting and even discouraging if coach and parents expect too much.

Other factors which influence losing may be that the swimmer made poor turns, was slow off the block, took a gulp of water, or was badly affected by the "wash" from the next swimmer's lane. Perhaps the water was too cold, and his muscles were not sufficiently limbered up. One of Shane's friends was excessively slow in a 400 medley swim and seemed to be pausing at each end of the 25m pool. He had forgotten to tighten the strings in his swimsuit, and was having a quick hitch at each turn to prevent them from falling off! Girls also need to be sure that their swimsuit fits comfortably—loose straps can be shortened with a few deft stitches, or tied back with soft tape or ribbon.

Reasons for losing are legion. But the fact which remains constant is that the winner is usually naturally talented and has put in some serious work at learning and practising his sport.

WORLD-RECORD BREAKER

The high point of competitive swimming is trying for a world record. To swim faster than any human being has done before in a given distance, to know that you have beaten not only the competitors in that particular race, but all the others who have ever gone before you, is the ultimate in personal satisfaction for a swimmer. Olympic medal wins are mixed with other emotions of team-spirit and national pride, but the World Record is superlatively individual.

This is a personal account of Shane's seven world-record swims from April, 1971, to January, 1972.

April 30, 1971. 100-metre freestyle. Crystal Palace, London.

Time: 58.9 sec

Split: 28.5 sec

In March, 1971, Shane had first gone "under the the minute" for the 100m freestyle in the New South Wales Girls' Secondary Schools Carnival, with a time of 59.7 secs, so she was hopeful of bettering this in her first international competition.

The trip to London, the first stage of a European tour by 12 Australian swimmers, brought out some very excited anticipation in Shane, especially the hope of meeting and competing with the world's fastest sprinter for 1970, Gabriele Wetzko of East Germany. The prestigious meet, a beautiful stadium packed to capacity, world TV coverage, and the responsibility of swimming for Australia hit Shane with great solemnity and set her tingling with determination to do well.

Her swim of 58.9 sec, equalling Dawn Fraser's world record (made in 1964) rocked the swimming world. Her coach had not expected her to reach this goal until she was 16 years of age, and I personally felt it was practically sacrilegious to set one's cap at the great Fraser's record! Like most Australians, I had believed the Fraser exploit would stand for all time. For a 14½-year-old schoolgirl to match this achievement was unbelievable. Further, it seemed to confound the coaching experts who believed that good distance swimming was easily within the capacity of a young swimmer, but that sprinting was the province of the mentally and physically mature.

For Shane, the swim had one defect. Two other competitors in the same race had failed to activate the electronic timer at the finishing touch, so the race was timed manually (as was Dawn Fraser's). However, there was a discrepancy between the electronic (59.102) and the manual time, so Shane felt that although she was close, she did not really own the record. Her main pleasure in the result was that she had improved by at least 0.6 sec on her previous best time.

May 1, 1971. 200-metre freestyle. Crystal Palace, London.
Time: 2 min 06.5 sec   Split: 1 min 01.9 sec

The day following the 100m record, Shane set her sights on competition with the American, Debbie Meyer, triple Olympic gold medalist, and at that time current world-record holder of the 200m. (Karen Moras had broken her 800m record the year before and the 400m record the day before.) Not knowing that Debbie was out of form, Shane put all she had into the race, and in clocking 2 min 06.5 sec, nipped 0.2 sec off Debbie's record.

Press and TV, alerted by her swim of the night before, turned out in force. The race was filmed and shown around the world many times in the following weeks. The newspapers featured a tearfully happy young girl who waved spontaneously to the crowd in acknowledgment of their cheers, which had encouraged her on to the record.

(Looking at her stroke in that race, it is interesting to

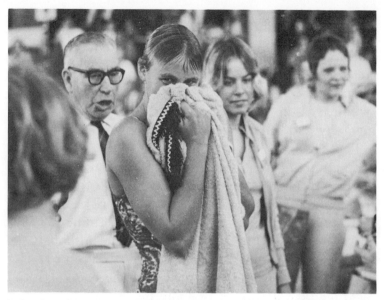

In London after she set a world record in the 200 metres, clipping 0.2 sec off the previous record. Shane shyly hears the announcement, tearfully happy.

note that her recovery then was more round-armed, whereas a year later her elbows in the recovery position had become higher.)

Shane was interviewed by the media for a long time after the race. In fact it took so long that she had to go back to her hotel room alone—the other swimmers had left to get ready for a dance that evening. After the incredible excitement of achievement and the adulation of crowd and press, this physical loneliness completely overwhelmed her, and she threw herself onto her bed for an old-fashioned sobbing session. Half an hour later Brad Cooper found her and persuaded her to come and join the party.

A week later, reading her letter 13,000 miles away, I was jolted into realizing what the Crystal Palace experience had meant to her—a 14½-year-old—giving an adult performance in a completely adult situation, unable to share either the joy or the weight of her triumph with close family, the very excellence of her achievement setting her apart from others. Never before in her young life had she been more isolated and alone, and never before had she been more completely her individual self. That night in London was a milestone in maturity for Shane.

July 9, 1971. 400-metre freestyle. Santa Clara, California.
Time: 4 min 21.2 sec
Splits: 1 min 03.8 sec
2 min 09.6 sec
3 min 16.4 sec
4 min 21.2 sec

The 400m was on Shane's fifth day in Santa Clara, and by then she had established a very warm relationship with the Ciabattari family with whom she was staying. Gene and Marian and their five children drew Shane right into their family in those few short days, and the thought of departure the next day made them all wish the stay could be longer. So Shane, and Janet and Lori Ciabattari made plans to have an extra day for sightseeing in San Francisco. Not really wanting to extend the visit, her father nevertheless said playfully to Shane, "OK, an extra day in California if you get the world record in the 400 metres."

Racing conditions were perfect on that cloudless July day: the pool was exactly the right temperature (78°), the competitors were world class, the spectators in their crowds were very responsive to the exciting performances, the announcers and the board for the electronic timing kept everyone informed of the progress of the races. Interest was also heightened by the presence of a very strong Soviet team of swimmers. Add to this, a determined youngster who badly wanted to win her father's bribe, and up came a world record which clipped 1.4 sec from Karen Moras' mark set at the Crystal Palace three months before!

November 26, 1971. 200-metre freestyle. Drummoyne
Pool, Sydney.

Time: 2 min 05.8 sec

Splits: 1 min 01.4 sec

2 min 05.8 sec

This swim took place at one of the Top Level Meets
arranged by the New South Wales Swimming Association to enable swimmers to qualify for entry in the
winter and summer championships. These meets are
somewhat pedestrian affairs and are regarded solely as
a means to enable hopeful swimmers to qualify under
correct procedural conditions, with registered officials.
Apart from the swimmers and officials, the only spectators are parents or friends who have acted as chauffeurs
for the competitors. Their main interest is to see their
child swim, collect the official timekeeper's card, and
get home as quickly as possible.

The races are conducted on the basis of best times
submitted on the entry forms—slow heats first, fastest
one last. An "under 10," an "under 12" and a 16-year-
old could feasibly swim in the same heat if their times
were in the same range. Later, ribbons are awarded to
1st, 2nd and 3rd in each age group when the race times
for all the heats are recorded. There are no finals.

On this particular Friday, Shane went to morning
training at 4:45 a.m. and complained about feeling
rather lethargic and slow. She went to school for the
full day, had a grilled steak and salad at 4:30 p.m.,
and took herself off for a sleep. The meet was to begin
at 6:30, and normally Shane would have arrived at
5:30 for a warm-up, but, realizing that she had had a
long day, I didn't waken her until 6 p.m. and then
offered her the choice of swimming or staying at home
watching TV. She sleepily decided to go to the pool,
so when she and her father set off I rang a friend at the
meet and asked her to put Shane's entry card in.

At the pool she "warmed up" by using her small

exerciser about 15 minutes before she was called to the marshalling area. The night was pretty cool, the water barely 70°. On the blocks getting ready for the start, she felt as if she would lose balance and false-start, so she rocked backwards on her heels ready to take up her position again, and the starter's gun went off! All the swimmers hit the water before Shane dived in. The referee asked for the false-start rope to be lowered, but it stuck! By the time it was released all the swimmers were clear, and Shane was well out in front, swimming as if her life depended on it.

The 100m "split" of 61.4 was well noticed by the onlookers (all parents of the swimmers), as interest and excitement mounted. The cheering grew as Shane came out of the last turn and had 50m to go. The time of 2 min 05.8 sec astonished her. "I felt so ashamed at being left behind on the blocks that I just put my head down and went!" was her explanation.

December 3, 1971. 800-metre freestyle. Drummoyne Pool, Sydney.

Time: 8 min 58.1 sec

In this race, during the week after the 200-metre swim, Shane was matching herself not so much against the competitors in the pool, as against the record set by Anne Simmons, the outstanding American, who had been the first woman to "go under" 9 minutes for this event during a race in Minsk, Russia. Here are the times Shane was trying to beat:

Shane's Splits:		Anne Simmons' Splits:	
1 min 03.3 sec	63.3 sec	1 min 03.0 sec	63.0 sec
2 min 10.5 sec	67.2 sec	2 min 10.5 sec	67.5 sec
3 min 18.4 sec	67.9 sec	3 min 18.0 sec	67.9 sec
4 min 26.3 sec	67.9 sec	4 min 26.4 sec	68.0 sec
5 min 34.7 sec	68.4 sec	5 min 35.3 sec	68.9 sec
6 min 43.2 sec	68.5 sec	6 min 43.2 sec	67.9 sec
7 min 51.9 sec	68.7 sec	7 min 51.8 sec	68.6 sec
8 min 58.1 sec	66.2 sec	8 min 59.4 sec	67.5 sec

An added incentive that day was the fact that old friends, Lew Hoad of tennis fame and his wife Jenny, were on a brief visit to Sydney and had come along to watch.

Reminiscing with Lew, Shane happily helped eat his meat pie and tomato ketchup (that great Australian stand-by at sporting meets). While matching him bite for bite through the spicy, sloppy meat encased in pastry, she suddenly found herself summoned to the marshalling area.

With the worst pre-race meal ever eaten, and her thoughts filled with plans of staying in Spain at the Hoads' "Campo de Tenis" after the Olympics in Munich, it was small wonder that Shane found her 800-metre race a hard one!

The week afterwards, Shane received a letter of congratulations from Anne Simmons—a rather warm gesture of good sportsmanship. If only these two girls had swum the race together, what a thrilling spectacle it would have been—and one cannot help wondering what the result might have been!

December 12, 1971. 1500-metre freestyle.

Birrong, Sydney.

Time: 17.00.6

Splits:

1.05.8	6.49.2	12.30.1
2.14.7	7.57.8	13.38.5
3.32.9	9.05.9	14.47.0
4.32.3	10.14.3	15.55.1
5.40.7	11.21.6	17.00.6

The 1500m "world record that wasn't" was swum at the Winter Nationals in Brisbane in September, 1971, on the same day as the American National Championship was holding its 1500m for women. In bettering Debbie Meyer's time of 17 min 19.9 sec by 0.4 sec, Shane was said by the officials to have set a world record, and everyone was jubilant. That is, until the newspapers next morning carried the story that Cathy Calhoun, only 13 years old, had in fact taken the record the same day in the better time of 17 min 19.2 sec! Shane had been beaten by 0.3 second!

The next opportunity came three months later at the Time Trial series. By this time, Shane was receiving considerable publicity and people were starting to wonder if it would be possible for her to make the 1500 her third world record in three weeks.

The race was held on a Sunday evening, in the Olympic Pool of Birrong, in the western district of Sydney. Mr. and Mrs. Suburbia, plus all their children, turned out in full force. Pyjama-clad toddlers mixed with grandparents who had just come from their game of lawn bowls, and there was a large sprinkling of young folk with hair still wet from their afternoon swim. The small stand was packed, children sat cross-legged on the pool concourse, families ate pies and sandwiches on the green lawns. Journalists and TV crew were on hand, amateur photographers were at the ready, excitement and anticipation ran high.

The 1500 is normally a boring race. This one had the stop-watch buffs calculating every lap and the spectators all watching every stroke. Swimming strongly with precise assurance from the very start, Shane made that race undeniably hers. She was completely overwhelmed by the timekeeper's announcement of 17 min 00.6 sec— no less than 18.6 sec better than Cathy Calhoun's. "It didn't feel so fast—it just felt easy" said a very delighted girl afterwards. Then she added, "I think it may be my last 1500. I really don't like the distance."

The race took a toll of Shane. A week later she was still getting over both the physical effort of the swim and the recognition of it. She had innumerable interviews, received over 100 fan letters, along with requests for personal appearances at fêtes and TV shows, besides being occupied with end-of-the-year school plays and other activity. Even with the family's protection and a change to an unlisted telephone number, she found this a week to look back on, not to live through again. By the next week-end, her physician advised complete rest, and in two days she slept 30 hours.

January 8, 1972. 100-metre freestyle North Sydney Olympic Pool.

> Time: 58.5 sec
> Split: 28.8 sec

After the 1500 race came Christmas, and Shane spent the time until the New Year staying with our family at her grandparents' beach house, 60 miles north of Sydney. With the New South Wales State Championships on from January 7 to 15, she kept up a training programme, although it was on restricted lines.

The 100m freestyle was scheduled for the opening night of the championships. A fine, warm evening brought crowds never before seen at the pool. Officials were literally overwhelmed by the pressure of the crowds—the stands were filled to capacity, standing room was likewise filled and approximately 3,000 people were turned away. Many subsequently walked on the footway of the Sydney Harbour Bridge which towers over the pool, and had a bird's eye view of the races from 500 feet away. As a family, we were embarrassed to be told that this crowd had come specifically to see Shane swim the 100m, and it was no secret that everyone had paid their money to watch a world record being set.

TV coverage had been planned, and in order to get live transmission of the women's 100 into a convenient time slot, it was brought forward before the men's 100. All the men in the race chivalrously agreed to let the ladies swim first. Shane, thinking she had another 15 minutes before racing, was quietly working away on her exerciser in a small storage room. She was found there by an official and asked to come for the race, as

"Why didn't they tell me?" Shane is asking through her tears, as she comes to the blocks for the start of the re-scheduled 100 metres in January, 1972.

the others were already at the blocks. Taken unaware, feeling unprepared, she was bewildered by the request, and asked "Why didn't they tell me?" Tears started to well up, but she brushed them aside, took a few deep breaths, pushed her hair up under her cap rather more slowly than usual, and came to the blocks looking solemn and half-crying.

Over the first 25 metres, she appeared to be stroking rather slowly, and comments of "she didn't go out fast enough" could be heard. At the 50-metre turn, she flipped over and the touch time of her feet was 28.8 sec. On the return lap, she surged ahead to the roars of the crowd, her stroking got faster and stronger, her shoulders lifted out of the water, and she touched the wall at 58.5 sec.

Of all the record swims, this was the one she wanted most.

PROGRESSIVE RECORD

100m freestyle times in 50-metre pools

Jan. 1967 (age 10)	1 min 18.3 sec	(Sydney)
Jan. 1968 (age 11)	1 min 08.3 sec	(Sydney)
Jan. 1969 (age 12)	1 min 05.7 sec	(Rockhampton, Queensland)
March 1970 (age 13)	1 min 01.9 sec	(Brisbane)
Jan. 1971 (age 14)	1 min 00.3 sec	(Hobart, Tasmania)
Feb. 1971 (age 14)	59.7 sec	(Sydney)
April 1971 (age 14)	58.9 sec	(London)
Jan. 1972 (age 15)	58.5 sec	(Sydney)

WHEN TRAINING TIME SHORTENS

Swimming-training is the means to the goal of producing good times in the racing season, especially in the summer. However, because of the many commitments to racing days, training miles drop off and top condition gradually peters out, so that by the end of the racing season (2 months for Shane) it is considered a minor miracle if her times can approximate those at the beginning of the season.

These three months, from January through March, 1972, in addition to being physically extending, also were emotionally exciting. She was acclaimed in newspapers around the world as Sportswoman of the Year, she attended two very prestigious evenings in Sydney when she was presented with a trophy as "Australian Sports Star of the Year" and "Sportsman of the Year" respectively.

Shane and Grahame Windeatt being interviewed by the press and broadcasters at the Sydney airport on returning from the European tour in May, 1971.

Her afternoon training sessions were preceded by interviews with French, German, Italian, Russian, American and British journalists—not to mention the Australians—and many training sessions were photographed. Unsettling and time-consuming as this may appear, it was less worrying to Shane to be interviewed and photographed with her squad than to make appointments for the journalists at home when she needed to rest.

When people comment to me that Shane must lead a very limited life because she spends all her time at swimming-training, I realize that they have no idea of how wide her experiences really are. Already a veteran world traveller, she has become adept at handling press and TV interviews. She has also learnt to turn public appearances into occasions for personal enjoyment. Meeting other sporting personalities, ambassadors and mayors is helping her to participate in community affairs. She is also gaining experience with public speaking, and discussing varied topics with older people.

Shane's life is very much enriched simply because she spends so much of her time swimming up and down a pool!

Shane with Karen after the European tour during which they became very friendly rivals.

9. The Triangle: Parents - Coach - Swimmer

When parents have decided to undertake swimming for their Johnny Hopeful, they are faced with the matter of choosing a coach. In some areas there may be no choice, and the decision may then lie in giving the coach a trial, or "doing it yourself" with the aid of a good book! Where choice is possible, parents should use their opportunity intelligently, enquiring carefully into the coach's credentials.

A good coach should have a certain quality of humanity about him—an empathy with his swimmers in their search for personal excellence in their sport, and a contentment in seeing himself as a catalyst, not the recipient of another person's achievement. With this basic personality, he will surely put his skills of teaching and his knowledge of human behaviour to good use.

A young coach starting out should ideally work with an established squad, learn the routine, ask a great many questions (and listen well for the answers), attend every possible seminar on swimming, see every film, subscribe to every swimming magazine, and read every authoritative book. As there appears to be no College for Swimming Coaches he should do his utmost to educate himself.

It is to be hoped that eventually there will be such a college in Australia—or anywhere. Graduates from this would then insist on professional standards when applications are called for new coaching concessions at Municipal Council Pools.

The best man to choose is an established coach who

has a full programme for all stages of swimming—from learning-to-swim, through stroke development groups and distance-conditioning to fully advanced. He will have a systematic plan for stage-by-stage learning, and the young swimmer can tell by his promotion from one group to another just how he is shaping up. Programmes will be different for each level of development: fast swimming is inappropriate for those whose stroking is not yet correct, and distance is not suitable for those who have not yet mastered the "bubbling out under the water" method of breathing.

There are enormous variations amongst the men and women who are involved in swimming coaching. But some of the factors common to all good coaches are:

1. A conviction that their methods are right for the swimmers who come to them for training.

2. A sensitivity to any changes in their swimmers' performances and sufficient interest to enquire about the cause.

3. A genuine desire to train their swimmers to their optimal capacity for competitive performance.

4. A willingness to work along with club officials.

5. Iron self-discipline for the long and irregular hours of work and the necessity to keep fit himself.

It is essential for a swimmer to feel completely confident and respectful of his coach. Shane has had extremely good and happy relationships with her coaches; she has worked on this, it hasn't been merely fortuitous. In her day-to-day contact, she has found it best to tell a coach before the session starts if she has a cold, a sore shoulder or leg muscles, so that allowance can be made for poorer effort. (Complaining about soreness just when a hard programme is announced is somewhat suspicious of malingering. Bringing it up at this point causes an interruption to the programme for other swimmers in the group, and this disruption is not appreciated!) Shane has always sought her coach's advice if she has felt some kind of fault developing in her stroke. A quick inspection by the coach if warranted can prevent hours of wrong stroking, or nagging doubt.

At the age of 9, she regarded her first Australian coach (Ken Wiles) as a substitute father, but by the time she came to Forbes Carlile there seemed to be less of a generation gap and more of a feeling of junior and senior partnership in the business of promoting a skill.

Forbes Carlile was an Olympic pentathlon competitor, a lecturer in physiology, and is an inveterate experimenter and researcher. His contribution to Australian (and world) swimming is not always fully recognized, as he has no copyright on his lectures to coaching forums, on his letters to the editors of swimming journals, his research papers, and even his "Bulletins to Advanced Swimmers." His squad's success is due mainly to his ability to train and inspire other very competent coaches to work with him, and his willingness to change, modify and shift emphasis in training as new knowledge becomes available.

In fact Shane has had up to 40 per cent of her training sessions with the other coaches, like Henry Vargner and more especially Tom Green. Each one has a different approach to coaching and an individualized assessment of the swimmer's performances. Their combined resources provide a very well balanced teaching programme for the squad. Occasionally a personality clash occurs, and it is then easy for a swimmer to plan his sessions so that he is with the coach he gets on with best. Coaches as well as swimmers can have their bad days!

The log book also provides an excellent basis for the coach to observe the individual pattern of training needs for each swimmer. Because Shane has kept her log book consistently, her coach is able to know what seems to be right for her best performances. It is to

Carlile's credit that he is prepared to accept the evidence of Shane's log book in making reassessments of some of his previously held ideas of swimming training.

Carlile's wife, Ursula, has provided up till now the supplementary attention to detail and organization in their swim schools, as well as the intensive work necessary with the intermediate squads before they graduate to the advanced group. Her selection as Assistant Olympic Coach for Munich 1972 gives her recognition as a thoroughly competent, informed, experienced and dedicated coach.

PARENTS

Because pools and coaches are not always situated conveniently for every swimmer, parents can become very involved in the basic business of "getting the kids to the pool." Involvement on a deeper level occurs, because they are paying the coach, and they want to get value for their money! This desire for value is double-sided: parents have high expectations of both the coach's ability and of their child's response. In this triangular relationship it is easy to predict that if parents are disappointed in the child's progress, they will blame the coach before doubting their child's ability to learn, or their own unrealistic ambitions for him or her.

Sometimes it is realistic to doubt the coach's knowledge, ability, or methods of working with swimmers. In Australia, anyone who feels like it can call himself a swimming coach, and if his advertising is sufficiently plausible, and he can lease a spot at a pool, he is "in business."

There is a point at which a child should be responsible for his actions. If he agrees with his parents' idea of swimming-coaching, then it is up to him to make the most of

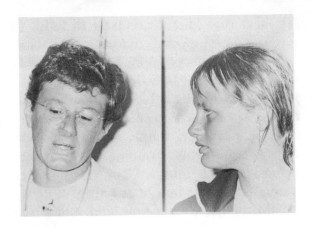

Shane discusses a problem with Ursula Carlile, Assistant Coach of the Australian 1972 Olympic team.

his opportunity. Doing his best should be his aim, and less than 90 per cent effort is not good enough in competitive sport. Admittedly, giving of his best will depend largely on the planning of the swimming programme, and the teaching ability of the coach, but if that is good then it is up to the child. Those who have been "softies," indulged or pampered, now have the chance to overcome these traits. The swimmer will be exposed to a whole new learning experience, based on cause-and-effect and mastery of co-ordination with insight into self-discipline. Parents reflecting over the progress of a child's first year at swimming-training should look for and recognize that this kind of growth has occurred and that it can be credited to swimming!

Growth may not be steady but may happen in forward- and backward-moving stages. Parents are needed to encourage the forward move, and arrest the backward one. If a youngster cannot finish a day's programme, it may be because he genuinely feels unwell, has a headache, or is suffering from the coldness of the water. Forcing him back into the water may possibly work with some children, but most will respond better to a rub-down and a sympathetic attitude. Tell him he has not failed permanently, that this is only a temporary sèt-back, that he can try later to finish the session, or give it a go tomorrow, and try to stay with it longer.

These comments apply only to the child who really does desire to be in swimming-training. The one who is in it only to please his parents should be doing something else of his own choice.

Some swimmers simply haven't got what it takes to go through regular training. Some react against it by being late, not finishing laps, having extended visits to the bathroom, or in a multitude of little ways managing to disrupt the programme and annoy the coach. The onus is then on the coach to decide whether: (a) the programme is right for that swimmer; (b) the swimmer's health needs investigation; or (c) if parents should be advised to withdraw him altogether.

Sometimes the programme can be adjusted to suit an individual swimmer. For instance, an outstanding backstroker, hopelessly unco-ordinated for breaststroke swimming but being directed to swim the 800m Breast, may predictably try to avoid this discomfort, and he should reasonably hope for an alternative. Fewer sessions or a period of once-a-day sessions could be arranged for those who cannot take intensive training.

Swimmers are usually generally healthy, but in adolescence imbalances can occur in their physiological make-up. Often a low blood hemoglobin level has been the cause of a swimmer's inability to stick to the programme. A physical check can avoid many a flare-up of bad behaviour.

As coaches are a commercial commodity, they are reluctant ever to say "Your Johnny Hopeful is really hopeless. Get him into another activity." Yet morally, this is what coaches should be prepared to say! Swimming competitively does have a limited life-span, and giving up regular training sooner or later is always tacitly expected by everyone in it.

PARENTS' AMBITIONS

Ideally, a coach needs a "third eye" to know from the start just how much and what sort of pressure a parent will put upon his child; to what extent the child is realizing his own, or his parents' ambitions; and how far the parent sees the child as an individual in his own right, or a mere tool of his parents' search for ego-gratification.

Some children begin to swim purely for health reasons. Asthmatic and bronchitic children benefit enormously by the lung strengthening provided by swimming. The joy of achieving a physical skill is also high on the positive list for health-seeking children. An ingredient of talent, a character trait of determination, and an ambitious outlook could even make the once-weak child a champion.

Some youngsters are frankly pushed into swimming by parental fascination for a swimming hero, and their desire to have a duplicate in their own home. This can occur in a very obvious, forthright way (in which case the child knows exactly why he is being pushed!) or it can be subtle, veiled, indirect and mixed with strange motivations so that the child may readily be confused by the whole exercise. Even with so bad a beginning, a child may find that swimming is his "thing" and he may have considerable success at it.

It happens rarely, to be true, but some parents publicly berate or even slap their child for swimming poorly and losing a race. Competitive sport can be a worthwhile experience for both generations only if plain common sense and emotional maturity are maintained. Obsessive demands for winning and petulant mortification in losing have no place in competitive swimming.

Parents should assess realistically both their child's talent, and his ability to handle regular, organized training. This should be a happy, satisfying experience; an opportunity for recreational outlet; an exercise in physical co-ordination; a promotion of health, fitness, strength and growth; and it should all happen within a social atmosphere of cameradie and interest-sharing.

Every one of these "positives" holds true for Shane. She would not be involved in training for competitive swimming otherwise.

OFFICIALS

Surrounding the triangle of parents, coaches and swimmers, is the circle of officials who organize the sport of swimming. Without a framework of conditions, standards and rules, and the people to administer them, swimming would be only a diversion, not a sport.

The officials, men and women, undertake a task which has few direct rewards. Mostly it consists of long hours at a meet, straining eyes over a stop-watch, writing up records, checking competitors against entry forms, and hovering at pool's edge to check turns and the correct execution of strokes. They provide their own white clothes, and blazers, pay their own way to and from the pool, endure the finishing splash of cold water on their legs, the sunburnt nose of a hot day, and the merciless assault of rain in wet weather.

Many officials were once competitive swimmers, who discharge a debt of gratitude for the good old days, by giving time and knowledge to their sport. Others are parents of swimmers who feel interested enough to study and take examinations in order to become officials, and keep competition alive.

None would keep on with this voluntary task if he did not enjoy the swimming scene, or enjoy the personal relationships of this rather exclusive "club." Some hope for rewards of travelling as officials with a team of swimmers. In Australia, the selection of a manager for a touring team always has a prior claim to the choice of a coach. Only in very recent years has Australian swimming realized the necessity of having a professional coach to accompany a team. This has of course been a point of differing opinion between the coaches on the one hand, who feel that only they can understand the whole needs of the swimmers, and the officials who look to trips as rewards for services rendered.

Officials are the whipping boys when decisions on places, correct strokes and correct finishes are disputed. Occasionally an official's eye may not be quick enough to detect a swimmer's touch as he turns. One of Shane's friends suffered from having such a rapid turn that the judge missed seeing it; yet the strength of his propulsion from the wall left no doubt that he gained this from a beautiful push-off. Shane was disqualified in her first competitive breaststroke swim at the age of 9. Swimming in the centre lane at night in a poorly-lit pool she had to surrender her first place for "foul swimming" (dropping one leg). Coach, parents and swimmer on that occasion were extremely disappointed.

Breaststroke touches have been a recent source of local contention. Some officials rule that only a touch at the water-line is permissible; others (particularly those who attended meets overseas) are adamant that grasping the top of the pool's edge to facilitate the turn is perfectly allowable. While the dispute raged several swimmers were disqualified, including an outstanding little 10-year-old, for whom encouragement and not rejection was surely needed. Many onlookers to this situation have wondered what was the motivation of interpreting a rule to make breaststroke more difficult for Australians than for the rest of the world!

In the main, however, officials at all levels, from the local club to the national body are people who are dedicated, and far from self-seeking.

What does a swimmer do on holiday? Go to the beach, of course. Here, Shane and her sisters are enjoying themselves at Yamba on the NSW North Coast after receiving a Civic Welcome by the Mayor of Grafton. (This photo is from the Grafton newspaper.)

10. Living with a Champion

Shane has a deep sense of the seriousness of her swimming. We may try to make her take it more lightly, but she refuses. Swimming is very definitely her thing. Quietly competitive, "being the best" is very important to her. "When will she rebel against it?" people ask, but this question is really irrelevant because she has regulated her own discipline so that rebellion would only amount to changing her own mind.

Murray Rose observed at Santa Clara that "Shane is more focussed on what she does, than any other swimmer I have ever known." This is a very interesting and revealing comment from a man who fascinated a previous swimming generation with his champion's personality.

It's great to live with a champion. Our whole family enjoys the brush-off from Shane's achievements; it makes us more identified as a family unit, and more cohesive in spirit. We also feel deeply satisfied about hard work being worthwhile as Shane is living proof of the truth of the equation

$$Talent + Training = Achievement + Reward.$$

This truth is easier to accept when the family finds her generous-hearted, cheerful, enthusiastic, willing to help, and a thoroughly delightful person to live with.

On her side, Shane probably gains from being a member of a family which is large by today's standards. She is not the only one doing fascinating things, and she is very happy to share her sisters' interests and listen to their successes and problems.

Swimming is an interest common to five out of six of

us: Lynette teaches beginners, Shane, Debbie and Jenny are in the training squad, and my husband Ron, a strong swimmer in his youth, now time-keeps at meets and has unlimited patience for watching races. My hopes for my daughters ran along the lines of ballet classes and music lessons, but the children made their choice, and I was swept along by their enthusiasm. I still read all the swimming books and magazines, enjoy the association with the coaches and the other parents, and am completely convinced that swimming has been a truly beneficial activity for my children. Quite apart from the social fun, the physical strengthening, and the mental toughening of training and competition, swimming has been the cure we needed for Jenny's annual bronchitis.

My role as a swimming mother involves, besides driving children to the pool, trying to keep a balance between swimming demands and the general needs of the family, being watchful over the diet and rest, and lately, acting as Shane's secretary! In this latter rôle I have had to say "no" as graciously as possible to most of the invitations she has received for competition overseas, for receiving awards and making personal appearances in places as distant from Sydney as Paris and Puerto Rico. Ron and I regard Shane's commitments in this order: School and home first—sport next—the world at large, third.

Success and recognition have come so quickly to Shane that we are still rather surprised by it, and we have certainly not incorporated it into being part of our normal life. We do discuss with her the likelihood of fame being fleeting and awards being history, and she recognizes very well that she will not always continue to hold records she has broken. Shane speaks in terms of "I mustn't let it go to my head" and Ron repeats "Let's just keep it all in perspective." Then

Shane at 14 months enjoyed her inflatable ring. The photograph does not show a very watchful father ready to rescue her if necessary. Had we known then how easy it is to teach a baby to swim, Shane certainly would have learnt without artificial support.

Shane at age 4 was swimming in Fiji. Here she is on the right and Lyn on the left with me in a muu-muu.

Debbie makes us all laugh by spontaneously putting on a pop-star act, holding an imaginary microphone and shouting "Here I am, fans—don't cheer, just throw money!"

Values within a family circle can afford to be different from those of the world outside, so the family can give equal recognition to Lynette's good essay on "Antony and Cleopatra," to Debbie's election as captain of her netball team, to Jenny's star for good work at school, and Shane's latest world-record swim. One evening over dinner we discussed with equal concern, Shane's invitation to Paris to accept the Sporting Academy's Award, and Jenny's problem of finding homes for her increasing number of guinea pigs.

Our household routine runs fairly smoothly, and everyone feels responsible for her own room and belongings. Busy families need organization, but fortunately we don't feel squeezed into a pattern which exists for the sake of keeping the house tidy. The routine is accepted so that we all can fit in our activities within the limits of a busy seven-day week.

Even the younger girls have a good notion of planning the time available to them, and they like to know ahead what the coming weeks hold for them. The responsibility of getting to practice on time is shared equally between us; the girls get ready and say when they want to go. I do the driving.

Rest is a vital part of training, and we regard it as a positive contribution to enjoying the next day. We never regard rest negatively as being just absence of activity. Shane still needs supervision over bedtime—this is the only area where her self-discipline falters. Her resolution is probably poor because of physical fatigue at the end of the day. With her own personal daylight saving arrangements, bedtime must be between 7:30 and 8 p.m. so that she can begin the next day at 4:30 a.m.

Shane looks to her father, Ron Gould, for approval. Here she is 11 years old at the North Sydney Pool.

At that early bedtime the co-operation of the rest of the family is necessary—noisy radio or TV programmes are not allowed close to Shane's room, and the rest of the family accepts this with tolerant resignation.

There are some occasions when Shane has desperately needed sleep, but thoughts of exciting days ahead, or even a mentally stimulating book prove too much for sleep, so I sit with her and put her to sleep through a method of modified hypnosis. Using a flat, slow, monotonous voice I go through the patter: "Your foot is relaxed and tired and ready for sleep. It feels heavy, weary, wanting to rest. Your leg is relaxed, and tired and ready for sleep . . ." and so on, dealing with all parts of the body up to the head. The slower and more monotonous, the better. This can take as long as ten minutes, but often it takes less. It is very important for both the would-be sleeper and the sleep-inducer to

regard the whole thing very seriously and be completely uninhibited about it. A giggle can disrupt it completely.

Sleeping during the day is essential at championship times, when heats are held in the morning and the finals at night. Shane prepares for sleep by darkening her room as much as possible, wearing her pyjamas, and getting into bed between the sheets. If there is noise outside—neighbourhood children playing, sounds from traffic—she switches on an electric fan close to her bed, but facing away from her. In this way, the humming sound of the motor cuts out the outside noises, yet the cold air from the fan doesn't bother her.

FEEDING THE CHAMPION

In our family, food and eating together have always been a source of daily interest and pleasure. The evening meal is particularly looked to with relish, and is almost always preceded by remarks such as, "I'm starved, Mum, when's dinner?" Food has never been withheld as punishment in the family; nor has anyone ever been forced to eat anything, or made to "sit there until you finish it." We hardly ever have angry scenes at the dinner table—meals are calm and enjoyable times together.

I have always offered new food to the family with the encouragement to taste it, as well as to smell and look. There is no fuss if it is turned down by one, but enjoyed by another. We are all entitled to be individuals and individual taste is respected.

Every schoolgirl these days knows about the importance of a "balanced diet" and eating from each of the main food groups each day. In the Gould household, these groups are:

Protein foods: For growth—meats, fish, eggs, cheese, lentils and nuts.
Vitamin foods: For good health and body function—fruits and vegetables.
Carbohydrates: For energy—sugar, bread, potatoes, and cereals of all kinds.

Food keeps more of its value if it is eaten fresh, or raw, or as nearly as possible to its natural state. Fresh orange juice has more food value than orange jam; whole-grain bread has more vitamins than refined white bread; raw vegetables have vitamins which are lost in cooking, etc.

In our family it is not necessary to urge the children to eat something "because it is good for you." They have been conditioned to liking the foods which are the best promoters of health. Pies, puddings, French fries, cakes and cookies do make their appearance, but they are not constantly "on the menu."

Some of our regular food habits are:
- Eating mostly whole-grain bread
- Adding wheat germ to breakfast cereals
- Using honey as a substitute for sugar
- Cooking potatoes in their jackets (or adding chopped parsley to compensate for the loss of Vitamin C when they are peeled and served mashed)

- Using fresh fruit for dessert
- Eating nuts and dried fruits as snacks, or in school lunches.

We try to avoid animal fats, and add made-up powdered skim milk to whole milk. We use brown rice in preference to polished white rice.

Shane's diet before she was three was fairly typical of the average Australian infant. Daily she drank up to 30 oz. of milk, had one egg, one or two small servings of meat and three vegetables; she ate sandwiches with a concentrated yeast-extract spread or honey, and had orange juice and one or two pieces of fruit.

When she was three, our family moved to Fiji—those beautiful islands some 2,000 miles north-east of Australia —and there we found the local food a real delight. We bought all those fabulous tropical fruits and vegetables from the local market, and the mangoes we had growing next to the house provided weeks of chin-dripping abundance. I belonged to a multi-racial Women's club, and by exchanging recipes and calling on my knowledge of food values, I managed to give my children a very good, healthful diet in those six marvellous years.

Returning to Australia, the whole family missed the unlimited availability of tropical fruits, but they gradually settled for the seasonal stone-fruits and dried fruits from the store.

Until she was 14, Shane's lean frame carried no excess fat. Her very active life encouraged a healthy appetite, and the growing process used up the calories when activity didn't. But when her growth eased off at 14, it became apparent that she would have to be more selective about eating, so the obvious calorie-carriers of bread, potatoes and corn had to be reduced.

Now Shane's diet is simple but varied. Perhaps she eats less quantities of meat than some athletes do, but

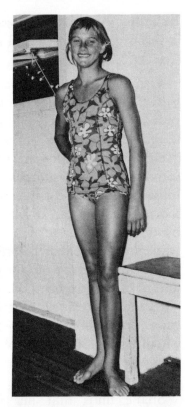

Unlike other girls her age, Shane's busy training schedule and watchful diet seldom allow for leisurely snacks like this—ice cream soda and French fries—with a group of friends.

A low-fat, high-protein diet helps to keep Shane slim and strong. A sample of one day's menu is as follows: BREAKFAST: orange juice; Muesli cereal (rolled oats with dried fruit and nuts) with hot skimmed milk or cereal with banana, wheat germ, honey and milk; one poached or pan-scrambled egg; toast and tea. SCHOOL LUNCH: tomato stuffed with cottage cheese, one apple or one orange, snack-pack of nuts and dried fruit. DINNER: roast lamb with mint sauce, baked potato and pumpkin, zucchini (green squash), peas, or string beans, fresh fruit salad, glass of skimmed milk.

she eats fewer steamed puddings, pies and pastries than the average Australian girl. Her sweet tooth sometimes leads her astray towards candy!

Shane takes Vitamin C, and Vitamin B complex daily, with Vitamin E added during very heavy training. She takes a course of iron tablets 2 or 3 times a year.

KEEPING HEALTHY

Some special precautions are necessary to keep swimmers free from the infections passed on at pools.

First, ears . . . After each swimming session, Shane puts 2 or 3 drops of a dilute methylated spirit (alcohol) preparation into each ear, after first going through head-shaking motions to get all the water out. Using the "spirit" ear drops regularly has avoided the nuisance of sore ears, in fact, she has enjoyed three years of swimming without an ear infection. Some swimmers who are more prone to ear infections can get extra protection by using a smear of petroleum jelly in each ear, for a waterproofing effect before going into the water. The Spirit ear drops dry out the ears, toughen the membranes and also kill any bacteria.

Feet are also susceptible to effects of water. Frequent examination of the skin between the toes is essential to watch for the beginnings of "athlete's foot." Commercial creams or powders are most effective if used when the small eruption first occurs.

Shane finds that her *hair* has thinned and been bleached by the combination of chlorinated water and sunshine, so she uses a conditioning cream on it after shampooing. She has also been wearing a bathing cap more frequently since she noticed the adverse effect on her hair, and this is improving the situation.

Skin loses its natural oil by being soaked in water, and Shane finds that regular applications of baby oil are necessary to avoid unpleasant dryness.

Using *eye-goggles* is another small aid especially for a really long session. The effect of chlorine in pools varies with the weather, as well as with occasional human error, and sometimes swimmers can experience a painful smarting of their eyes. Eye drops are helpful after the swim, but some of the effects can be avoided by wearing goggles, especially if they fit snugly around the eye socket. Tinted goggles are a boon when swimming in very hot, bright sunshine.

OVERTRAINING

Having a champion in the family is an opportunity for friendly and well-meaning people to offer congratulations and proffer advice. The most frequent advice given by elderly folk is this: "Don't let Shane burn herself out." They fear that hard training may cause her permanent physical damage, but I think they are quite mistaken. Swimmers become fatigued, but this is only temporary. The so-called "burnt-out" swimmer is more likely to be suffering from a damaged ego or a broken heart. I suggest that the pattern leading to this condition is as follows:

- Interest in training flags
- Race times get slower
- The swimmer feels he would like to give up
- Pressure is applied by parents and coach, and he feels obliged to keep on with it for the sake of others
- He trains resentfully
- He puts no heart into his effort
- His performance drops
- He feels guilty about letting others down
- He feels ashamed about being beaten
- He ends up taking "refuge" in genuine or psychosomatic illness.

When he is ill, people then say he has burnt himself out.

The start of this unhappy sequence is the flagging interest in swimming-training. Anyone associated with the sport will agree that keeping a swimmer interested in training is like trying to harness an elusive but very powerful force. The whole gamut of motivational

Shane has all the normal home life any girl wants, including a pet beagle, Libby.

psychology could be called into service here. The fact, too, that swimming is so individual a sport means that pressure and stresses cannot be shared with a team, but must be borne alone. But the swimmer is also a social person, and his social environment is of great significance to him. Coaches, parents, the social climate of school and pool, even national attitudes are all important in creating for the swimmer the total personal environment in which he will be encouraged or discouraged in his interest in training. When the personal environment is negative, the top-class swimmer has to rely completely on his own inner resources, and these can get worn away over a period of time.

Reverting to Shane: Interest in swimming has been no problem for her. It comes as a natural corollary to having success at an activity she has chosen and which she loves. There is no need to deliberately contrive interest. But she has also been fortunate in having a total environment which is positively conducive to sustaining her interest.

First, her relationship with her coaches has always been excellent, and her response to them has in turn increased their eagerness to help her. Perhaps she has been less demanding on her coaches than some swimmers, because she does not rely completely on their judgment, expect miraculous guidance, or infallible advice. She shares equally with her coach the responsibility of deciding what is best for her.

Next, her school. Turramurra High School, under the leadership of Harry McDowell, has given Shane exceptional support in staying with her swimming. Maybe the school is accustomed to champions, as Gail Neall (selected for the Australian team in Munich) and Jimmy Carter, an outstanding young swimmer, also attend the school. Mr. McDowell and his staff have given special attention to the needs of these athletes: Shane arranges for her friends to take carbon copies for her of notes missed. In seeking out her teachers for directions for "catching up" she finds that they go out of their way to be helpful. Moreover, the school takes great pride in all their students' extra-curricula activities and recognizes their achievements at the school assembly. The students, like Shane, really feel keen to do their best at the regular school subjects because of their acceptance as respected citizens of the school community.

Last, home environment. Frankly, we are not an aggressively competitive family, but we do believe in "the search for excellence." For myself, I am dedicated to the goal of seeing my children develop to the maximum of their basic abilities. The words of the old hymn

"Just as I am, young, strong and free,
To be the best that I can be,"

have very special meaning to me. Within the family, the children are not compared with others—they are only measured against the yardstick of themselves. At the risk of being branded sentimental, my favourite quote is "This above all—to thine own self be true." Live up to your own self-image is perhaps a more modern expression of the same idea.

When young, Ron listened weekly to his father's sermons. A Methodist minister, he most used the text "no man having put his hand to the plough, and looking back is fit for the kingdom of heaven," and he coined the word "stick-at-ive-ness" to impress the sermon on the children of the congregation. As an adult, Ron believes strongly in living each day to the fullest—he has no retrospective yearnings, no wasted laments on "what might have been." With a background of Welsh pride, he sets high standards for himself and for his family. When his daughters find the going hard, he encourages them on with this little piece of doggerel—

> Somebody said it couldn't be done,
> But he with a chuckle replied,
> That even if it couldn't,
> He would be one
> Who wouldn't say so till he'd tried.
> So he buckled right in
> With a trace of a grin
> On his face. If he worried he hid it.
> And he started the thing that couldn't be done,
> And what do you think? He did it.

Working for 25 years in the airline industry, Ron has visited most countries of the world, and has come home impressed with qualities of other races and nationalities. The perseverance of the Germans, the incredibly diligent application of the Japanese schoolchildren, the ingenuity and grit of the Americans, the reverence for perfection in European culture, and the strength of family bonds in the Fijians have all impressed him. These values are older ones than Australians have had time to develop, but Ron has tried to incorporate them into his thinking and his outlook, and into the quality of our family life. He is concerned that as Australians we are too often afraid or embarrassed about excellence

Shane, greeted by her sisters—Lynette (standing), Debbie (left), and Jenny (right)—at the airport in May, 1971, when she returned from Europe.

—it is far more comfortable to be "average." But for our family, searching for excellence is a way of life, and Shane Elizabeth Gould has already found it.

NOTES

1500 metres (30 laps of a 50m pool) is known as a "metric mile" for racing.

In training, 32 laps or 1600 metres is what counts as a mile.

A true mile is 1,760 yards, or 32 laps of a 55-yd pool. 1600 metres is roughly 1,733 yds. Times set in a 55-yd pool are better than the same time in a 50m pool.

Long course in Australia means 50-metre or 55-yd pool.

Short course means 25-metre pool.

There are no 25-yd pools used for racing in Australia.

SHANE'S READING LIST

Johnny Weissmuller: "Swimming the American Crawl" (1930) (Putnam)

Forbes Carlile: "Forbes Carlile on Swimming" (1963) (Pelham Books)

Rose Marie Dawson: "Age-Group Swimming" (1965) (Pelham Books)

Don Talbot: "Swimming to Win" (1969) (Pelham Books)

Harry Gallagher: "Harry Gallagher on Swimming" (1970) (Pelham Books)

James Counsilman: "The Science of Swimming" (1968) (Pelham Books)

Magazines

   The Swimming World (U.S.A.)
   The Swimming Times (U.K.)
   The International Swimmer (Australia)

Index